JOHN DRYDEN

JOHN DRYDEN

BY

DAVID NICHOL SMITH

THE CLARK LECTURES ON
ENGLISH LITERATURE
1948–9

ARCHON BOOKS
1966

FIRST PUBLISHED 1950 BY
THE SYNDICS OF THE CAMBRIDGE UNIVERSITY PRESS

REPRINTED 1966 WITH PERMISSION
IN AN UNALTERED AND UNABRIDGED EDITION

LIBRARY OF CONGRESS CATALOG CARD NUMBER: 66-20232
PRINTED IN THE UNITED STATES OF AMERICA

CONTENTS

Preface   *page* vii

   I. Early verse and Criticism   1

  II. Plays   23

 III. Satires and Religious Poems   44

 IV. Translations, Odes, Fables   67

Index   91

PREFACE

These four lectures on 'John Dryden of Trinity College' were delivered, one a week, in the University Lecture Rooms, Cambridge, in October and November 1948. Though they are now printed as chapters in a little book with the addition of a few footnotes, they still remain lectures.

It is a pleasure to me to acknowledge the privilege of speaking about Dryden on the invitation of the Master and Fellows of his own College, and I wish also to thank them, and the Master in particular, for the kindness shown to me on the four visits when as Clark Lecturer I was their guest.

D. N. S.

MERTON COLLEGE
OXFORD

I

EARLY VERSE AND CRITICISM

One of Dryden's early poems bears the signature 'J. Dryden of Trin. C.' It was published in the year of his admission, and it was the only poem that he published as an undergraduate. We know very little about him while he was here, and indeed our information about him at any time, beyond what may be learned from his own writings, is surprisingly scanty. He appears to have left Cambridge on taking his bachelor's degree. His master's degree was conferred on him several years later at Lambeth. But he remains John Dryden of Trinity College.

Politics and the theatre were to bring him into closer association with Oxford, especially in the days of the Exclusion Bill, when parliament held its brief session there. Altogether he addressed no fewer than eight prologues and epilogues to the University of Oxford— not by any means the happiest efforts of this great master of the prologue, but of interest in their criticism of the London stage and their praise of the opportunities presented in a home of learning for the performance of the legitimate drama. In these prologues Dryden set out to please his academic audience, and to the end of his life he was never on oath when he meant to please, no matter whom. On hearing of the success of his first prologue he said in a private letter 'how easy 'tis to pass anything upon an university, and how gross flattery the learned will endure'. The flattery grew in grossness and reached its climax when he contrasted Oxford with his own mother university. But a year or two later when he wrote his 'Life of Plutarch' he had no occasion to flatter anyone; and in this Life—which as a critical essay deserves more attention than it seems to receive—he went out of his way to recall the days when he read Plutarch in the library of Trinity College and to add, with manifest sincerity, 'to which foundation I gratefully acknowledge a great part of my education'. This brief acknowledgement tells us more of his life at Cambridge than we learn from the college record of his gating for disobedience to the Vice-Master, or from the rumour which was raked up in his later life of his discomfiture at the hands of a young nobleman on whom he had written verses. Dryden was as good a Greek scholar as any English poet between Milton and Gray, and he had not learned all his Greek under Dr Busby at Westminster.

We in our turn are under an obligation to members of this college for their work on Dryden, and to two of them in particular—W. D. Christie and A. W. Verrall. After Malone with his unexcelled capacity for research had collected the material for our biographical and explanatory accounts of Dryden, and after Walter Scott had brought out his great edition and furnished it with what is still the most readable life, little work was done on Dryden for about fifty years. Roughly in the twenties of the last century, even while Keats was discovering him, Dryden entered on the period when he suffered more neglect than at any other time. But in 1870 there appeared the Globe edition with these words on the title-page, 'edited with a memoir, revised text, and notes, by W. D. Christie, M.A., of Trinity College, Cambridge', and also with these words—'Glorious John Dryden'.

This book has been a stand-by to students of Dryden in our time, the edition to which many of them have turned first as a matter of course, and I gladly take this opportunity of acknowledging my debt to it. Verrall's *Lectures on Dryden* likewise represent a stage in Dryden studies. We are told that as soon as he was appointed to the new chair of English in this university he decided to inaugurate it by speaking on Dryden, because of his long-standing admiration, and with a mind to correcting the neglect which he found among his younger friends. He did not live to complete his lectures for publication; but the vigour and the acuteness of the portions which survive for us to read show how he must have aroused his hearers. No one can say now that Dryden is neglected. Verrall's *Lectures*, delivered in 1911 and published in 1914, are at the beginning of the new interest in him which keeps on growing.

We may adopt new lines of approach to Dryden, we may consider new aspects of his work, but we cannot easily ignore his historical setting. He is so much a child and a representative of his age that without some knowledge of this setting a great part of his work would lose much of its meaning. There have been many books written on Shakespeare that never mention the Spanish Armada, or the Church Settlement, or the Union of the Crowns, but we cannot read Dryden without learning, whether we will or no, something of the political history, and something of the religious history of his times, and religion then was closely knit with politics. But some knowledge of history, however desirable or even unavoidable, takes us only a short distance in the study of a poet, or a critic. It can never explain his quality or account for his pre-eminence.

3

When Johnson in his edition of Shakespeare was dealing with plays of doubtful authorship he spoke of the triple test of 'the diction, the versification, and the figures'. In this apparently simple remark he pointed the way to a recent development in criticism, for by 'figures' he meant what we now call 'imagery'—and what student of English literature is not familiar with the term 'imagery'? Criticism of Dryden has been advancing on each of these three lines. Studies of his diction we have been given, and others may be coming. We have studies of his versification. Now his imagery, in which he is richer than is commonly supposed, is winning attention. Criticism will continue to find new fields, and new ways of working them. And Dryden will continue to divide his critics. I doubt if any great English poet has aroused so wide a divergence of opinion.

To his admirers he is 'glorious John Dryden'. We owe the phrase to Scott. It is spoken by Claud Halcro in *The Pirate*, but Halcro was the mouthpiece of Scott himself. Not merely did he edit Dryden and write his life; he went out of his way in *Marmion* to speak of Dryden's 'God-given strength' and 'lofty line'. He was roused by the lift and the swell of the verse, and the tireless energy which never suggests an effort. I have already mentioned Professor Verrall. I might mention also Professor Saintsbury who invariably caught fire whenever he spoke of Dryden. But when I once said to Robert Bridges that Dryden was rightly called 'glorious John Dryden' he at once replied 'there is nothing glorious about him'. I did not know then that he had written an essay on Dryden—actually on Dryden's faults, which no doubt are many—and I still do not know why he wrote it, if not to proclaim his dislike. In this essay he says that

4

Dryden is 'a poet with whose works I am by choice unfamiliar'.

What divides his critics as much as anything, I believe, is that, in comparison with some other great poets, he appears to have skimmed along the surface of life. Those who do not like him think him lacking in moral conviction and settled outlook. He is not a poet who labours with deep and perplexing thoughts that must work their way into words. Even when he is in doubt, as he frequently was, his thought, to judge from his ease in presenting it, seems not to have harassed him for long. *He* could not have called himself a dedicated spirit, except in so far as he was dedicated to the literary profession and to good writing. Towards the end of his life he spoke of himself as 'a man who has done my best to improve the language, and especially the poetry';[1] it was that which he considered to be his strongest claim on the generosity of his country in the poverty of his old age. He never needed to be upheld by the belief that his rewards were to come when he was gone, that he was to leave behind him a work that posterity would not willingly let die. He lives in the present. He takes his part—a poet's part—in the controversies of the day, and in the celebration of national events. Rich as our literature is in poems on special occasions, from the death of Edward King to the funeral of the Duke of Wellington, no other great poet was more given than Dryden to finding his subject in what was happening, or had just happened. If he did skim along the surface of life, he had a great deal to say about it.

The occasion of his first notable poem was the death of Oliver Cromwell, and here he struck a chord that was to resound in his later work.

[1] Letter, 7 November 1699.

> His *Grandeur* he deriv'd from Heav'n alone,
> For he was great e're Fortune made him so;
> And Warrs, like mists that rise against the Sunne,
> Made him but greater seem, not greater grow.

In such a stanza as this Dryden announces himself. He is getting into the swing of the 'majestic march', to use the happy and familiar words of Pope—the march which can move rapidly over any ground. The whole poem is not all like this. It has its awkward corners when we are held up by obscurities or by unhelpful allusions. But even if we were not familiar with Dryden's later work, I do not think that we should fail to say that this poem has a quality unlike that of other poems written at the same time, and a quality which would make us wish to know more of the author. It was published as one of three poems on the death of Cromwell, another of them being by Edmund Waller. The reputation of Waller was then at its height, and Dryden regarded him as a master, but most of us will say that the poem of the novice is the better.

Two years later Dryden celebrated the Restoration of Charles II. His family were Cromwellians, and his admiration of Cromwell himself had been whole-hearted, but the country had been changing its mind during the intervening years of unsettled government, and Dryden, who by temperament was not a strong party man, hailed the return of the court as the return of the nation to a life of greater ease and richer colour.

> At home the hateful names of Parties cease,
> And factious Souls are weary'd into peace.

The most striking passage in *Astræa Redux* describes Charles's welcome by the crowds at Dover, but there are many happy couplets, as when he says of the Restoration

> 'Twas not the hasty product of a day,
> But the well ripened fruit of wise delay;

or when he speaks of the discontent of the younger people, in words which remind us how we often heard after the First World War (but not after the Second) that the lot of our younger people had been spoiled by the folly of their seniors:

> Youth that with Joys had unacquainted been,
> Envy'd gray hairs that once good days had seen:
> We thought our Sires, not with their own content,
> Had ere we came to age our Portion spent.

The faults noted in the earlier poem are disappearing, the thought is running clearer, but Dryden has not yet written a poem that moves steadily of its own momentum.

He had his own early work in mind when in middle age he wrote his poem to the memory of Oldham, who had anticipated him as a satirist but was still a roughish writer at his death at the age of thirty. In it he says—

> O early ripe! to thy abundant store
> What could advancing Age have added more?
> It might (what Nature never gives the young)
> Have taught the numbers of thy native Tongue.

He excuses the roughness of Oldham's verse by his youth; but he is not to be taken to say, as I fear he sometimes is, that no young poet is flawless in his metre. That would be, at the least, an overstatement. Young poets have written perfect lyrics. What he does say is that the writing of verse requires practice, and of no kind of verse is this more true than the kind employed by Oldham in his satires, and by Dryden in *Astræa Redux*—the heroic couplet. It is a difficult measure in which to win dis-

7

tinction. Even Pope, the most precocious of all its masters, found that advancing age taught him not a little about it. Now Dryden was not a precocious poet. He was almost thirty when he wrote *Astræa Redux*, and looking back on it and other early pieces twenty years later he was well aware of what he had learned in the interval.

Even his *Annus Mirabilis* was to show a gain in vigour and confidence rather than in technical skill. The Year of Wonders—the year of the Dutch War, the Plague, and the Fire of London—he thought the 'most heroic subject which any poet could desire', and it called for an effort. He admits that it cost him much trouble. Yet it may be called, I hope not too colloquially, a hit-and-miss poem. No reader of the rather tedious account of the fight with the Dutch can fail to have his attention aroused and held by such lines as these—

> The mighty Ghosts of our great *Harries* rose,
>   And armed *Edwards* look'd with anxious eyes—
>
> Silent in smoke of Canons they come on—
>
> His presence soon blows up the kindling fight,
>   And his loud Guns speak thick like angry men.

Or by this passage describing the beginning of the Fire—

> Then, in some close-pent room it crept along,
>   And, smouldring as it went, in silence fed:
> Till th'infant monster, with devouring strong,
>   Walk'd boldly upright with exalted head....
>
> And now, no longer letted of his prey,
>   He leaps up at it with inrag'd desire:
> O'r-looks the neighbours with a wide survey,
>   And nods at every house his threatning fire.

8

Or, when the Fire reaches St Paul's—

> The dareing flames peep't in and saw from far
> The awful beauties of the Sacred Quire:
> But, since it was prophan'd by Civil War,
> Heav'n thought it fit to have it purg'd by fire.

All this is true Dryden. Here is the characteristic throb, the full resounding line. It is passages such as these which his admirers remember at the mention of *Annus Mirabilis* But this 'heroic poem' was too comprehensive to be all written in a high strain of enthusiasm. Seeking for realism in his account of the navy he made the experiment of introducing nautical terms. 'I have never yet seen the description of any naval fight', he says, 'in the proper terms which are used at sea.' It was the first of his experiments in poetry, and let him be given credit for making it, though it failed. The proper terms as he used them removed the poem from the heroic plane. A display of detail in one stanza has invited the comment 'rather like an auctioneer than a poet'. And in the versification there are weaknesses. For example, the tricky little word *did* too often supplies a needed syllable.

The poem was accompanied by a preface in which he began the excellent habit, which he was never to abandon, of taking his readers into his confidence and telling them why he had written as he did, or what he had been thinking in the process of composition. In this preface he explains why he had reverted to the stanzas of four lines which he had employed in his Cromwell poem. The choice for him lay between this stanza and the couplet. We have to remember that *Annus Mirabilis* appeared in the same year as *Paradise Lost*, and that it was not till the

9

publication of *Paradise Lost* that blank verse, long
established as the verse of the drama, became one of our
great narrative measures. No poem of any length had
been written in it since Gascoigne's *Steele Glas*, and it has
never lent itself to the heroic treatment of recent events.
Nor did the Spenserian stanza enter into his choice, for it
was then out of fashion, as was likewise the stanza of
eight lines which had been used by the Elizabethan translators of Ariosto and Tasso; and the Chaucer stanza of
seven lines had barely survived the Elizabethan period.
It may still be a question which form of verse is best
suited to narrative, though the answer must depend on
the gifts of the poet. But Dryden's choice was small.
He chose 'quatrains or stanzas of four in alternate rhyme
because'—to quote his preface—'I have ever judged
them more noble and of greater dignity both for the sound
and number than any other verse in use amongst us'.
He was never at a loss for a reason. On this matter, as on
others, he may have changed his mind, for he was not to
write another poem in the same measure. None the less
he had shown its scope in 'sound and number' for the
celebration of stirring deeds, he had proved how it could
be used to 'sound the trumpet, beat the drums' of a
national rejoicing. For us it has very different associa-
tions. The stanza of *Annus Mirabilis* is the stanza of
Gray's *Elegy*, and we now think of it as the elegiac
stanza. It has had a varied history. In Elizabethan times
Sir John Davies had used it, and used it well, in his *Nosce
Teipsum* for a philosophical inquiry into human nature
and the soul, in which there is nothing heroic or elegiac.
Sir William Davenant in his long narrative poem
Gondibert made it heroic and descriptive with incidental
moralizings, and had set the example to Dryden.

Normally it has a slow movement which fits it for quiet musing, as the eighteenth century was to find. It was coming to be accepted as an elegiac measure before Gray claimed it. But towards the end of the century Johnson was to say in his *Lives of the Poets*—'Why writers have thought the quatrain of ten syllables elegiac, it is difficult to tell. The character of the elegy is gentleness and tenuity, but this stanza has been pronounced by Dryden, whose knowledge of English metre was not inconsiderable, to be the most magnificent of all the measures which our language affords.'

The *Annus Mirabilis* marked out Dryden for the laureateship, and when about a year later the post fell vacant no time was lost over his appointment. The 'warrant for a grant to John Dryden of the Office of Poet Laureate' was issued in April 1668 only six days after the death of Sir William Davenant.[1] This appointment has been confused with his appointment two years later as Historiographer-Royal; and delayed payments have added to the confusion by being taken to indicate an increase of royal favour. When Tennyson died in 1892 and his successor was not appointed for three years, some of us can remember hearing that there was a precedent for the delay in a two years' vacancy before the appointment of Dryden. In fact Dryden's appointment was unusually rapid—the most rapid in the whole history of the laureateship. No regular duties were attached to the office. It was the Hanoverians who expected every year the double salutation of a New Year's Ode and a Birthday Ode. Dryden was free to write as the occasion presented itself, and it did not come soon—not till after twelve years, during which he was occupied with the drama.

[1] *Calendar of State Papers, Domestic, 1667–8*, p. 341.

His appointment was as obvious then as after these twelve years it proved to be fortunate. Yet, as a poet, he had not yet quite found himself. It has to be admitted that we read the early poems in the light shed on them by the later. Even when he is at his best and gives us what he could never have bettered, we think of the poems which have made his fame. But already he was finding himself in prose. While he was writing his *Annus Mirabilis* he had begun his Essay *Of Dramatick Poesie*. That work stands on its own feet, and no allowances need be made for it. Had he written nothing else, that work alone would have secured for him his place among our great critics. It was the only critical work that he published by itself, for the great bulk of his criticism took the form of prefaces, and he thought it important enough to revise it carefully some years later for a second edition, in which the alterations affected only the phrasing, not the substance.

We do well to remember what we ourselves have experienced, and are experiencing, from the upheaval of two great wars when we try to picture how the country stood in the early days of the Restoration. Like ours it was a time of unsettlement that called for readjustment without any possibility of going back to what had been. New forces were coming into play, movements which had already begun were gathering strength. The advance of Science was in the Restoration mind as it is in ours.

Is it not evident, in these last hundred years (when the Study of Philosophy has been the business of all the *Virtuosi* in Christendome) that almost a New Nature has been reveal'd to us? that more errours of the School have detected, more useful Experiments in Philosophy have been made, more Noble Secrets in Opticks, Medicine, Anatomy, Astronomy, discover'd, than in all those credulous and doting Ages from *Aristotle* to us? so true it is that nothing spreads more fast than Science, when rightly and generally cultivated.

That has a familiar ring to us, but these are the words of Dryden. Much was hoped from the intellectual movement of the new age, which found a clear expression in the foundation of the Royal Society. But if the new conditions inspired optimism, they also brought a sense of uncertainty. In no branch of literature was doubt more obvious and more reasonable than in the drama.

If we were asked to name a good representative of the sceptical, inquiring attitude of these years, we should not do wrongly if we chose the Essay *Of Dramatick Poesie*. No one who comes to it after reading Elizabethan criticism, or the criticism of the earlier part of the seventeenth century, can fail to be aware of a new spirit. Wherein the newness lay cannot be better indicated than in Dryden's own words—

My whole Discourse was Sceptical, according to that way of reasoning which was used by *Socrates*, *Plato*, and all the Academiques of old, which *Tully* and the best of the Ancients followed, and which is imitated by the modest Inquisitions of the Royal Society. That it is so, not only the name will shew, which is *an Essay*, but the frame and Composition of the Work. You see it is a Dialogue sustain'd by persons of several opinions, all of them left doubtful, to be determined by the Readers in general.

He states contradictory views, and very fairly, as they are all tenable. If we suspect how his preferences lay, we note his freedom from the didactic manner which was common in earlier criticism, and indeed few of our critics at any time have habitually tried to preserve so open a mind. He has a problem, the drama itself has a problem, and it must be examined sceptically.

And the problem was this. The older English drama, the drama represented triumphantly by Shakespeare, and Beaumont and Fletcher, and Ben Jonson, has passed. It was a great drama, and we are proud to be in the tradition, but that is not the kind of drama which we need to try to write, for times and taste have changed. We have another great drama to consider, the drama which has grown up in France, and it is written on different principles. We may not like it, but we cannot ignore it; we may be well advised to take ideas from it, judiciously. Nor must we forget the third great drama, the drama of Greece and Rome, from which the French drama is in part derived. In comparison with these three great dramas the plays which we are producing are of small account. Yet the theatres have been full since their reopening on the king's return, and we are offered our chance, but how best can we take it?—That was the problem as Dryden saw it. In the plays which he had as yet written, he had been feeling his way with no clear aim. He had written a comedy in prose, which Pepys thought 'so poor a thing as I never saw in my life almost'. He had written a tragi-comedy mostly in blank verse, which Pepys thought a 'pretty, witty play'. He had collaborated in a tragedy wholly in rhyme; and then he wrote by himself a sequel to it, *The Indian Emperor*, which was successful. It was a new type of play, the heroic play as it came to be called. But he still had his doubts when the closing of the theatres on account of the plague gave him the opportunity to think about them, and he continued to think about them after the theatres were reopened and he had written a tragi-comedy in prose, blank verse, and rhyme.

If only to clear his own mind, he decides to write about the methods of the drama. He assumes the role of a committee of inquiry, collects the evidence, and delivers his report, and his report is the Essay *Of Dramatick Poesie*. No treatise of this kind had hitherto been attempted.

The last section of the Essay states the case for rhyme in the drama. We must bear in mind how dramatic blank verse had deteriorated in the seventeenth century. After Shakespeare had taken it to the limit of flexibility it tended more and more to lose its shape, and was often only rhythmical prose, when it was not stilted prose. As heard on the Restoration stage while Milton was writing *Paradise Lost*, it was a very uncertain measure. Concurrently with this deterioration the trend towards introducing rhymed passages had been strengthening and the experiment of writing whole plays in rhyme was to be expected. It may have been encouraged and hastened by the example of the French drama, but the way had been prepared. Keeping abreast of the times, as was his habit, Dryden adopted the 'new way' of writing, as it was called; he wrote *The Indian Emperor*. But controversy was inevitable, and he was not the man to stand aside. He chose the method of stating the case for blank verse as well as rhyme, and leaving the reader to decide for himself. He said the most for rhyme that could be said before he knew the argument, the conclusive argument, which was to be provided by experience.

One passage is of particular interest not merely because it shows why he favoured the innovation, but also because it has some likeness to what *we* have been hearing, and again I suggest that we shall understand the men of the

Restoration the better if we think of ourselves. The great Elizabethans, he says—

are honour'd, and almost ador'd by us, as they deserve; neither do I know any so presumptuous of themselves as to contend with them. Yet give me leave to say thus much, without injury to their Ashes, that not only we shall never equal them, but they could never equal themselves, were they to rise and write again. We acknowledge them our Fathers in wit, but they have ruin'd their Estates themselves before they came to their children's hands. There is scarce an Humour, a Character, or any kind of Plot, which they have not us'd. All comes sullied or wasted to us: and were they to entertain this Age, they could not now make so plenteous treatments out of such decay'd Fortunes. This therefore will be a good Argument to us either not to write at all, or to attempt some other way. . . . This way of writing in Verse [i.e. of writing plays in rhymed verse] they have only left free to us; our age is arriv'd to a perfection in it, which they never knew. . . .For the Genius of every Age is different; and though ours excel in this, I deny not but that to imitate Nature in that perfection which they did in Prose, is a greater commendation than to write in Verse exactly.

When we read this we are reminded of what our modern poets have been telling us. The case was stated for them, in part, in *The Times Literary Supplement* as early as 1912, in words as emphatic as Dryden's:

When a great master appears he so exhausts the material at his disposal as to make it impossible for any succeeding artist to be original, unless he can either find new material or invent some new method of handling the old. In painting and music this is almost demonstrable to the uninitiated; in poetry the law may not be so strict, but it still holds; and any one may see that serious rhyme is now exhausted in English verse, or that Milton's blank verse practically ended as an original form with Milton. There are abundant signs that English syllabic verse has long been in the stage of artistic exhaustion of form which follows great artistic achievement.

These are the words of Robert Bridges, who has been mentioned as being by choice unfamiliar with Dryden; but he has supplied a striking parallel to Dryden's argument about the exhaustion that follows great achievement; and in his poetry he sought for novelty of form, as Dryden did in the drama.

'The Genius of every Age is different.' There must be change. To honour the tradition is one thing, and to be content to follow in beaten tracks is another.

It was the pressing question of the verse of the drama that gave Dryden the idea of his Essay. He dealt with it last, but it had been first in his mind, before other topics of more lasting interest were combined with it in this sceptical discourse on the drama in general. If instead of dealing with it last he had decided not to deal with it at all, we should have lost an excellent discussion; but the Essay would have lost little or nothing of its significance in the history of our literary criticism.

While the condition of the English drama was Dryden's strongest incentive to write his Essay *Of Dramatick Poesie*, he was prompted to it also by recent publications, and by one in particular. Not by the *Short Discourse of the English Stage* by Richard Flecknoe, who was soon to be on the throne of dulness in *MacFlecknoe*. This *Discourse* was a waste of a good title, though it has remarks now and then which save it from being negligible. To Flecknoe's credit, it ends with the admission that it was written 'only to give others occasion to say more'; but no invitation was needed.

The recent writer to whom Dryden was under a real and undisguised debt was Corneille, and not more for the matter provided for discussion than for the stimulus given by a mind with which his own had much in common.

Dryden was well read in the dramatic criticism that derives from Aristotle's *Poetics*. He studied the *Poetics* of Scaliger. He knew the views of Heinsius and of Ben Jonson. How far he was familiar with La Mesnardière and D'Aubignac and the other French writers on the drama before Corneille is questionable. But all this criticism was summed up for him in the *Discours Dramatiques* which Corneille had added to the collection of his plays published in 1660. Here he found the methods of the French drama discussed with argumentative ease and clarity; and here he was provided with the incentive to join in the argument from the English standpoint. His comparison of the two dramas forms the central portion of the Essay. Nothing of the kind had yet been attempted in English, and as far as I am aware he was the first critic anywhere to attempt a comparison of two modern and living dramas. He gives us our first example, and an example that would have been very notable at any time, of what in our days has come to be called comparative criticism.

But criticism takes several forms. It may be concerned mainly with the principles of composition, with methods, with purpose, and how that is achieved. Briefly, the question before this kind of criticism is—how to write? But there is another question—how has an author written, what are the merits of his work? Dryden answered both in turn. Having discussed the methods of the French and English dramas he passed on to tell us what he thought of the great Elizabethans. He gave us our first deliberate estimate of them, and in so doing became our first great master of appreciative criticism.

Here again we can trace the interest which he had taken in Corneille's collected edition containing not only the

Discours Dramatiques but also Corneille's own 'Examens' of each of his plays. That a dramatist should write fully and frankly about his own work was a striking novelty; and it gave Dryden the idea of a different novelty. Why not an Examen of an Elizabethan play? He decided on an 'Examen of *The Silent Woman*'. The word 'examen' in the sense of a critical examination was not new in English, but its presence in this title was not accidental. The criticism of Ben Jonson's play extends to several pages, and is so full and rounded that it can be taken out of its setting and treated as an independent study. A comparable criticism of a single Elizabethan play was not to appear before the middle of the eighteenth century.

But it is when Dryden speaks of Shakespeare that the Essay comes to its apex. We know how Shakespeare had been praised since Ben Jonson declared him to be 'not of an age but for all time'. Dryden was not content with the ordinary topics of praise; his panegyric is not a mere condensation of what was in the air. Let me remind you that he makes a special point of Shakespeare's imagery:

All the Images of Nature were still present to him, and he drew them not laboriously, but luckily: when he describes any thing, you more than see it, you feel it too. Those who accuse him to have wanted learning, give him the greater commendation: he was naturally learn'd; he needed not the Spectacles of Books to read Nature; he look'd inwards, and found her there.

The imagery was an aspect of Shakespeare's art in which he was more interested than any previous critic appears to have been; indeed, I doubt if it is definitely mentioned anywhere in Shakespeare criticism of earlier date. Let me remind you also that he speaks of Shakespeare's faults,

19

even emphatically, but adds that 'he is always great when some great occasion is presented to him'. It is a balanced estimate. And it is a general estimate, not illustrated by the mention of even a single play or character, but concerned only with the qualities and features which distinguish Shakespeare from other dramatists. Its briefness—not three hundred words—did not allow of such detail as was to be expected in the 'Examen of *The Silent Woman*'. There the scope and the purpose were different.

And now let me quote what Samuel Johnson said of this great passage, after he had edited Shakespeare and written his Preface:

> The account of Shakespeare may stand as a perpetual model of encomiastick criticism; exact without minuteness, and lofty without exaggeration. ...nor can the editors and admirers of Shakespeare, in all their emulation of reverence, boast of much more than of having diffused and paraphrased this epitome of excellence, of having changed Dryden's gold for baser metal, of lower value though of greater bulk.

A remarkable passage, you will admit, from one who was not given to lavishing his praises, but Johnson knew the pedigree of his own preface. Dryden's Essay had struck the note and set the method of the best criticism of Shakespeare for the next hundred years. It was balanced, and it was general. In time we were to be told that 'general criticism is easy' (which it is not), and to find it replaced by the study of separate plays and their characters, and that was to be the main occupation of the critics till our own time. But here again Dryden had been before them in his discussion of the 'admirable plot' and the skilful drawing of character in Ben Jonson's *Silent Woman*.

The Essay has the vivacity of a good conversation in which the speakers pass easily from one point to another, and lighten the main discussion with remarks now and again on other matters. Before this dialogue came definitely to the questions which confronted the dramatist in the early years of the Restoration it had glanced at the changes which were taking place in poetry, and in prose. We find such observations as these:

Our Poesie is improv'd by the happiness of some Writers yet living, who first taught us to mould our thoughts into easie and significant words, to retrench the superfluities of expression, and to make our Rime so properly a part of the Verse, that it should never mis-lead the sense, but it self be led and govern'd by it.

Wit is best convey'd to us in the most easie language; and is most to be admir'd when a great thought comes drest in words so commonly receiv'd that it is understood by the meanest apprehensions, as the best meat is the most easily digested.

There is this difference betwext his [Cleveland's] Satyres and Doctor Donns, That the one gives us deep thoughts in common language, though rough cadence; the other gives us common thoughts in abstruse words.

(May I say in passing that this praise of Donne for giving us deep thoughts in common language has a striking likeness to a remark made by Coleridge in his Biographia Literaria—so striking that the remark may be an instance of unconscious memory.)

These passages might be taken as texts for the discussion of Dryden's own writing. 'To mould thoughts into easy and significant words', 'to retrench the superfluities of expression', 'to convey wit in the most easy language'—these were the aims of the poetry of the new

21

age, and of its prose. But I mention these passages now only as further evidence of the importance of this remarkable Essay.

To-day I have spoken of Dryden's early writing. In verse he was still teaching himself the numbers of his native tongue. In the Essay *Of Dramatick Poesie* he reached maturity.

II

PLAYS

In speaking of the Essay *Of Dramatick Poesie* I tried to show that it has a wider significance than its title would suggest. It struck a new note in our criticism by its impartiality in discussing opposite views and inviting its readers to come to their own decisions. It took account of the new conditions which had brought about a change in taste, and it glanced at the general movement in poetry. It gave us our first detailed examination of an Elizabethan play, and in its eulogy of Shakespeare it provided the model for the best criticism of him for the next hundred years. There is much more in this remarkably comprehensive little treatise. But it has one dominating characteristic. It looks forward, with the knowledge that a new drama has to be created—a drama that will remain in the English tradition, but with new features which will satisfy the demand for novelty, and more than that, will prove that the drama is alive by giving the best proof of life, by changing. The idea of change was continually in Dryden's somewhat restless mind. He had welcomed the new age. 'What has been, has been.' In the very last year of his life, when the new age had become an old age and had disappointed his hopes, he was to say: ' 'Tis time an old age is out, and time to begin a new.'

With the publication of the Essay he committed himself to the drama, and for the next twelve years he published nothing that was not connected with it. When Edward Phillips, the nephew of Milton, compiled his

Theatrum Poetarum in 1675 and included in it his English contemporaries, he began his account of Dryden thus—

John Driden, Poet Laureat, and Historiographer to His present Majesty: with whom such hath been the approbation and acceptance his Poetry hath obtained, especially what he hath written of Dramatic, with wonderful success to the Theater Royal...

and then he named several plays, and plays only. As a shareholder in the Theatre Royal in Drury Lane, Dryden had agreed to supply three plays a year. That was a sanguine promise, and was not to be fulfilled. Instead of three plays a year he wrote, on an average, about one. And he never settled down to one characteristic method or manner. French critics speak of 'le théâtre de Corneille' and 'le théâtre de Racine', and we may speak of the drama of Congreve. We cannot speak of 'the drama of Dryden'. We speak of 'Dryden's dramas'. One of them is a great drama, but taken together they show that they were not a wholly congenial medium.

He said as much in later life when he spoke of 'the stage, to which my genius never much inclined me'. He said it even while he was writing these plays, in the dedication of one of the best of them, his *Aureng-zebe*:

I desire to be no longer the *Sisyphus* of the Stage; to rowl up a Stone with endless labour (which to follow the proverb, *gathers no Mosse*) and which is perpetually falling down again. I never thought my self very fit for an Employment, where many of my Predecessors have excell'd me in all kinds; and some of my Contemporaries, even in my own partial Judgment, have out-done me in *Comedy*.

Dryden was a very good judge of his own work, and he was always frank about it. Unlike Corneille who goes back to his earlier pieces to discuss them methodically,

Dryden has a habit of telling us casually what he is thinking at the time of composition. His prefaces and prologues have the quality of studio talk in which the artist speaks of what he has tried to do, and how he has done better, or worse, than others. He gives us his views at the time; he may have different views at other times, but he gives us his views in relation to the work on which he is engaged. It is this quality of studio talk which accounts for the inconsistencies of which some of his critics have made too much. An experimenter such as Dryden was, and a very active experimenter, is not to be tied by old opinions expressed in different circumstances. His inconsistencies are more apparent than real and can generally be explained by a change in emphasis. That he should declare a preference for one method at one time was no reason why he should not try at another to make the best of the method which he had thought inferior. Or at one time he might concentrate on merits and at another on defects, according as the occasion invited him. The great point is that he always tells us what he is thinking, and tells us it with the freedom of conversation. There is no body of English criticism that is more alive, that brings us more directly into contact with the artist at work, than Dryden's prefaces. We cannot predict all the topics that will arise in the course of the conversation. 'The nature of a preface', he said, 'is rambling, never wholly out of the way nor in it'; but he never goes on a ramble without having something interesting to say, often about himself. In the passage which has just been quoted, he spoke of his unfitness for the drama at the very time when he was at the height of his reputation as a dramatist. He was finding that he had set out with too high hopes. The Restoration age was not producing a drama that could vie with the Elizabethan. As for himself, 'with the greater dead he dares not strive' and 'in a just despair would quit the stage'. None the less he was the leading dramatist of the decade from 1670 to 1680.

I do not propose to speak of his Comedies as he thought little of them. 'Neither do I value a reputation gained from Comedy', he says, 'so far as to concern myself about it, any more than I needs must in my own defence: for I think it, in its own nature, inferior to all sorts of dramatic writing. . . . I detest those farces which are now the most frequent entertainments of the stage.' And he suggests this reason: 'That I admire not any comedy equally with tragedy is, perhaps, from the sullenness of my humour.' We have to take his word for it that he was sullen, for he has not supplied the evidence on paper, though we have ample proof that he was apt to be quiet and retiring in company. What is certain is that he believed himself to be temperamentally unfitted for comedy. Yet he played his part with Etherege and Wycherley in shaping the Comedy of Manners, which can be traced back to the later Elizabethans and was to be perfected by Congreve. He thought *Marriage A-la-Mode* the best of his comedies, but very faulty. It comes most fully to life in the wit of the dialogue, in the skill of the thrust and parry. 'Repartee', he said, 'is the greatest grace of comedy, where it is proper to the characters', and with that in mind he wrote this play. It is not a long step to *The Way of the World*, where Congreve moves with greater ease and shows a lighter hand. When Congreve produced his first play, Dryden hailed him as his true successor. But Dryden's heart had not been in comedy.

His heart was, for a time, in the rhymed serious play. It gave him the opportunity of saying what he wanted to say and as he wanted to say it. We cannot read *Tyrannick Love* and *The Conquest of Granada* without seeing that they were an outlet for overflowing energy. The vigour with which they are sustained is remarkable. *Tyrannick Love* was written in seven weeks. The enthusiasm with which he wrote the first part of *The Conquest of Granada* carried him to a second—ten acts in all, and all of similar elevation.

> Poets, like Lovers, should be bold and dare,
> They spoil their business with an over-care:
> And he who servilely creeps after Sence,
> Is safe, but ne'er will reach an Excellence....
> He loos'd the Reins, and bid his Muse run mad:
> And though he stumbles in a full Career,
> Yet Rashness is a better fault than Fear.

So he said in the prologue to *Tyrannick Love*. *The Conquest of Granada* is more carefully written, but if he tightened the reins a little, and just a little, he never slackened the pace or changed the course. He meant it to be the great example of the Heroic Play, as indeed it is.

These plays invite us to remember that we should 'read each work of wit with the same spirit as its author writ'. We may have difficulty in adjusting ourselves to them, but Dryden has once again come to our assistance with a preface. He calls it 'Of Heroique Playes, An Essay', and he prefixed it to *The Conquest of Granada*. Its crucial statement is this: 'an heroic play ought to be an imitation, in little, of an heroic poem'. Whatever is admissible in the poem is admissible in the play. As the 'heroic poet is not tied to a bare representation of what is true, or exceeding probable', no more is the heroic dramatist. The characters, being heroic, are above the common human standard. Every drama is above our usual experience by reason of the selection that is necessary in an artistic presentation. As Congreve put it— 'the distance of the stage requires the figure represented to be something larger than the life. . . . I believe if a poet should steal a dialogue of any length from the extempore discourse of the two wittiest men upon earth, he would find the scene but coldly received by the town.' But Dryden goes much farther and assumes the liberty 'of drawing all things as far above the ordinary proportion of the stage as that is beyond the common words and actions of human life'. So much for the characters of the heroic play. He tells us that its subject is likewise controlled by its imitation of the heroic poem. He says explicitly that 'Love and Valour ought to be the subject of it'. Heroic love and heroic valour, both on the highest pinnacle to which they can be raised, and all presented in the most polished and sinuous couplets of which this master of the couplet was then capable.

Was rhyme necessary to the heroic play? Dryden does not say that it was. A strict interpretation of his words tells us that a play is heroic only by imitating an heroic poem, and does not rule out the possibility of an heroic play being written in blank verse; and a play that is written wholly in rhyme is not therefore heroic. We sometimes find the heroic play spoken of as a play in heroic couplets. That was not Dryden's definition. But rhyme was an attribute of the perfect type.

Once we understand the conventions of these plays we are in the fair way to enjoy them. We cease to be disturbed by the extravagances. We can imagine how passage after passage when declaimed by such actors as

Hart and Major Mohum won the applause of audiences that had not yet lost their taste for the *tirade*. Burlesque, in the cause of common sense, was easy, as the authors of *The Rehearsal* were to show; but Dryden had 'reason to be satisfied'—these are his own words—with the reception of his heroic plays.

It may be a question what he himself thought of the extravagances which reach and even pass the borders of the ludicrous—what he thought of them at the time of writing, for we know what he thought of them afterwards. Did he rely on his huffing actors to make them pass as heroic in the glamour of the theatre? This is Maximin in *Tyrannick Love*—

> My looks alone my Enemies will fright.
>
> If to new persons I my Love apply,
> The Stars and Nature are in fault, not I.

And (sitting down on the body of his assassin whom he has still strength to stab)—

> And after thee I go,
> Revenging still, and following ev'n to th'other world my
>   blow;
> And shoving back this Earth on which I sit,
> I'le mount—and scatter all the Gods I hit.

And this is Almanzor in *The Conquest of Granada*—

> No man has more contempt than I, of breath;
> But whence hast thou the right to give me death?
> Obey'd as Sovereign by thy Subjects be,
> But know, that I alone am King of me.
> I am as free as nature first made man,
> Ere the base Laws of Servitude began,
> When wild in Woods the noble Savage ran....
> Stand off; I have not leisure yet to die.

29

And here he is as the complete lover—

> Who dares touch her I love? I'm all o'er love:
> Nay, I am Love; Love shot, and shot so fast,
> He shot himself into my breast at last.

We will not believe that Dryden could have written such passages as these without a smile. Here if anywhere he must have meant to 'pit, box, and gallery' it, like Bayes in *The Rehearsal*. As one has to say again and again, he was a very good judge of his own work. He speaks of 'the rodomontades of Almanzor'. And we have to remember the prologue in which he says that he bid his muse run mad. He must have found some pleasure in writing these rodomontades, but there is no need for us to think that he took them seriously, nor that he meant them to be satirical. A few years later he made this public confession:

> I remember some Verses of my own *Maximin* and *Almanzor* which cry Vengeance upon me for their Extravagance.... All I can say for those passages, which are I hope not many, is, that I knew they were bad enough to please, even when I writ them: But I repent of them amongst my Sins; and if any of their fellows intrude by chance into my present Writings, I draw a stroke over all those Dalilahs of the Theatre; and am resolv'd I will settle my self no reputation by the applause of fools.[1]

The extravagances should not distract our attention from the serious element in these plays, which abound in observations on human nature as we all may know it. Dryden took the opportunity of writing about matters which were occupying his mind and were to occupy it for several years. I confess that I have found myself reading these plays without looking at the names of the speakers,

[1] *The Spanish Friar* (1681), Epistle Dedicatory.

and treating them not as dramas but as poems that carry
on an argument and are interspersed with remarks now
on one subject and now another. Dryden is continually
speaking of Fate and Fortune, of Faith and Reason and
Religion. Let me quote from *The Conquest of Granada*:

> O Lottery of Fate! where still the wise
> Draw blanks of Fortune; and the fools the prize!
> These cross ill-shuffled lots from Heav'n are sent,
> Yet dull Religion teaches us content.
> But, when we ask it where that blessing dwells,
> It points to Pedant Colleges, and Cells,
> There shows it rude, and in a homely dress,
> And that proud want mistakes for happiness.
>
> Ye Gods, why are not Hearts first pair'd above,
> But some still interfere in others Love!
> Ere each, for each, by certain marks are known,
> You mould 'em off in haste, and drop 'em down;
> And while we seek what carelesly you sort,
> You sit in State, and make our pains your sport.
>
> Reason was giv'n to curb our headstrong will.
>   Reason but shews a weak Physitians skill:
> Gives nothing while the raging fit does last,
> But stayes to cure it when the worst is past.
>
> By Reason, Man a Godhead may discern;
> But, how he would be worshipt, cannot learn.

All this leads on directly to *Religio Laici*, where Dryden
disburdened himself of much that had long been in his
mind. There are even verbal anticipations. In one of the
quieter passages of *Tyrannick Love* we read:

> Thus with short Plummets Heav'ns deep Will we sound,
> That vast Abyss where humane Wit is drown'd!
> In our small Skiff we must not launch too far;
> We here but Coasters, not Discov'rers, are.
> Faith's necessary Rules are plain and few.

Religio Laici tells us that

> The things we *must* believe are *few*, and *plain*.

Underlying all the extravagance and the bravura of the heroic plays we can trace a recurring and even continuous preoccupation with problems which were soon to come to the surface and demand open discussion.

None of his other plays is so rich as these are in maxims and moral sentiments, such as—

> Forgiveness to the Injur'd does belong;
> But they ne'er pardon who have done the wrong.

Everywhere we come upon the quotable passage—concise, pointed, final in its phrasing. In 1780, when Mrs Thrale was moved to express in her commonplace-book her fears for this country, which seemed to be hastening to bankruptcy and demolition, she quoted from memory two lines in *The Conquest of Granada* on the fate of empire:

> Then down the precipice of time it goes,
> And sinks in Minutes, which in Ages rose.

Dryden was still to write another tragedy in rhyme— *Aureng-zebe*. It is pitched in a lower key; the characters are of more ordinary dimensions; there is even an approach to domesticity such as Maximin and Almanzor never knew. We might not think of calling it an heroic play if we forgot its relationship to the more exalted members of the family. Dryden was then beginning to tire of rhyme. So he tells us in his prologue. He also tells us that

> What Verse can do, he has perform'd in this,
> Which he presumes the most correct of his.

This is his admission that he had been schooling himself in the numbers of his native tongue, and that he was aware of improvement. Good as is the verse in *Tyrannick Love*, it is not so consistently good as in *The Conquest of Granada*; and he thought it still better in *Aureng-zebe*.

No writer of the couplet has been more aware than he was of the monotony to which it is liable, or saw more clearly that if monotony is to be avoided there must be variation of rhythm *within the line*. As the subsequent history of the couplet has shown, this variation is not easily maintained in a poem of any length. There was good reason for Keats, before he knew Dryden, to speak of 'swaying about upon a rocking-horse'. There are various methods of avoiding the sway. You may run on the sense from one line to another, you may be content with a half-line now and again, or you may introduce alexandrines, or triplets. All these devices Dryden employed. But it was in the disposition of the stress within the line that he made his greatest contribution to the technique of the couplet.

To illustrate his variation of the rhythm we cannot do better than take the famous passage in *Aureng-zebe* where the hero in his adversity muses on the false promises of life—a passage which was much better known throughout the whole of the eighteenth century than it is now, and is probably the most famous passage in all his plays. The caesura, in English versification the pause in the middle of the line dictated by the sense, does not come in two successive lines at the same place.

> When I consider Life, / 'tis all a cheat;
> Yet, fool'd with hope, / men favour the deceit,
> Trust on, / and think to morrow will repay:
> To morrow's falser / than the former day;
> Lies worse; / and while it says, we shall be blest
> With some new joys, / cuts off what we possest.

> Strange couzenage! / none would live past years again,
> Yet all hope pleasure / in what yet remain;
> And, from the dregs of Life, / think to receive
> What the first sprightly running / could not give.
> I'm tir'd with waiting / for this Chymic Gold,
> Which fools us young, / and beggars us when old.

When the central pause is emphasized by coming regularly about the middle of the line, we get two halves which balance monotonously, we get the rocking-horse. We may even get what has been called a crease down the middle of the page. But not in Dryden.

Before I pass on from his rhymed plays let me ask if they ever remind us of an earlier writer. Who was it who wrote this?

> It lies not in our power to love, or hate,
> For will in us is over-rul'd by fate.
> When two are stript long ere the course begin,
> We wish that one should loose, the other win;
> And one especiallie doe we affect
> Of two gold Ingots like in each respect.
> The reason no man knowes, let it suffise,
> What we behold is censur'd by our eies.
> Where both deliberat, the love is slight,
> Who ever lov'd, that lov'd not at first sight?

Marlowe of course, in *Hero and Leander*.

> It lies not in our power to love, or hate,
> For will in us is over-rul'd by fate.

If we were asked where these lines come from, it would not be a bad error if we said *The Conquest of Granada*. Is it too fanciful to think of *Tamburlaine* as an early heroic play, written long before the heroic drama was thought of, and in less sophisticated times? Marlowe's hero was not caught in the toils of love, as the Restoration hero was bound to be, but the two heroes resemble each other in their 'conquering sword' and their 'high astounding terms'. Dryden knew *Tamburlaine*. Almanzor boasts that

> The best and bravest Souls I can select,
> And on their Conquer'd Necks my Throne erect;

and another boast which removes all doubt that he knew is it

> I'll cage thee, thou shalt be my *Bajazet*.
> I on no pavement but on thee will tread;
> And, when I mount, my foot shall know thy head.

There is no question of imitation or direct relationship. The likeness is due to the nature of the subjects, and also to the nature of the writers. I detect a Marlowesque quality in Dryden now and again, but his energy lacks the attraction of Marlowe's youth, he is more conscious of what he is doing, and he did not live in the spacious days of Elizabeth.

But there is nothing Miltonic in *The State of Innocence or The Fall of Man* beyond Milton's own words and ideas. It was an attempt to reduce the reducible matter in *Paradise Lost* to the formalities and elegances of a rhymed play, with the help of additional matter for which *Paradise Lost* gives no warrant. Written hastily for a court performance in honour of the marriage of the Duke of York and Mary of Modena, it was to have been, as the stage directions show, highly spectacular, but it was never performed; perhaps the 'Fall of Man' was not thought to be the right choice for a wedding celebration. Copies passed about in manuscript, and one of them must have fallen into the hands of Andrew Marvell, who expressed himself very forcibly in verses prefixed to the second edition of *Paradise Lost*. The inaccuracies of the manuscripts compelled Dryden in self-defence—so he tells us—to publish it, when it was accompanied by a dedication to the Duchess of York which is unpleasantly fulsome, and by a fighting preface called 'The Author's Apology for Heroique Poetry, and Poetique Licence'. Perhaps the best that can be said for this so-called Opera—which is not a libretto but a short drama with opportunities for music and dances and scenic effects—is that we should think better of it if we did not know *Paradise Lost*. For an examination of it, as penetrating as it is impartial, we shall not do better than turn to Verrall's *Lectures*. And I have the additional reason for passing it by in these brief talks, that my main concern is with what seems to me to matter most in the work of Dryden, with the qualities and features to which he owes his fame. But I go out of my way for the moment to say a word on his relations with Milton. 'The nature of a preface is rambling', and why not of a lecture?

His admiration of *Paradise Lost* was constant; in so far as it changed, it increased. It was an unlucky moment when he conceived the idea of what musicians call a variation on the theme. In his preface he says that *Paradise Lost* is 'undoubtedly one of the greatest, most noble, and most sublime poems which either this age or nation has produced'; and he is reported to have said in conversation that 'this man cuts us all out, and the ancients too'. These two prose statements are to be preferred to the verses about 'Three poets in three distant ages born' which he wrote for the first folio edition of the poem. But we know very little about the personal relations of Milton and Dryden. For this there are three pieces of evidence. The best known is provided by John Aubrey in the notes which he jotted down 'tumultuarily' (they make a very ragged manuscript) and sent to Anthony Wood. Aubrey there adds Dryden's name to a short list of Milton's 'familiar learned Acquaintance' and tells the familiar story about tagging his verses:

Jo: Dreyden Esq. Poet Laureate, who very much admires him: and went to him to have leave to putt his Paradise-lost into a Drama in Rhyme: Mr Milton recievd him civilly, and told him he would give him leave to tagge his Verses.

And he also says this about Milton:

He pronounced the letter R very hard   a certaine signe of a Satyricall Witt   from Jo: Dreyden.

We have to ask how Aubrey knew what was said at the meeting, or that there had been a meeting. Dr Verrall thought the story 'probably apocryphal'. But Aubrey may have got it from Dryden himself. He acknowledges that it was Dryden who told him how Milton pronounced R. Instead of writing about Dryden's life, Aubrey left a blank page, and said 'he will write it for me himself'—which Dryden never did.

The story is confirmed and supplemented by the second piece of evidence, printed in the periodical called *The Monitor* in 1713:[1]

We shall here beg the Readers Pardon for mentioning a Passage told a Gentleman of our Society almost Forty years since by Mr *Dryden*, who went with Mr *Waller* in Company to make a Visit to Mr *Milton* and desire his Leave for putting his *Paradise Lost* into Rhime for the Stage. Well, Mr *Dryden*, says *Milton*, it seems you have a mind to *Tagg* my Points, and you have my Leave to Tagg 'em, but some of 'em are so Awkward and Old Fashion'd that I think you had as good leave 'em as you found 'em.

[1] No. 17, 6–10 April 1713: pointed out by G. Thorn-Drury in *The Review of English Studies* (January 1925), Vol. 1, p. 80.

Again we do not know who supplied this version of the private conversation. The mention of Waller does not make it any the less credible. It may well have been Waller who introduced Dryden to Milton.

The third piece of evidence comes from Dryden's own preface to his *Fables*: '*Milton* has acknowledg'd to me, that *Spencer* was his Original.'

All this evidence does not take us far. It certainly does not prove that Dryden was one of Milton's 'familiar learned acquaintance'; and Aubrey's other words 'went to have leave' and 'received him civilly' point in a different direction. There may have been only one visit, but if there was only one, Dryden made very good use of his chances. He got Milton to talk, listened attentively to his R, and, above all, led him to speak of his debt to Spenser. Clearly they got on well—Dryden admiring and curious, and Milton not uninterested, perhaps a little cynical, but courteous and talking at his ease. This may all have happened in one visit, and if there were half a dozen (which is improbable) I imagine that their relations remained much the same. We must, I think, conclude that they were 'familiar' only in so far as Milton was willing to receive Dryden—unlike Hobbes, with whom he would have nothing to do.

But Dryden's admiration of Milton did not extend to the early poems, in which the rhyming word did not seem to him to come spontaneously enough. 'The rhyme', he says, 'is always constrained and forced, and comes hardly from him.' As far as I am aware, Dryden has nowhere made a criticism of an English author that is more difficult for us to understand. When he points out Shakespeare's faults we understand him, whether or not we agree. We understand him when he says that much of

Shakespeare's wit is out of fashion. But our ears are not attuned to finding any trouble with Milton's rhymes. Much the same distinction is drawn by Johnson between *Paradise Lost* and the early poems. Johnson thought that in *Lycidas* 'the diction is harsh', and that the songs in *Comus* are 'harsh in their diction and not very musical in their numbers'. Perplexing observations! Many people brush them aside by saying (wrongly, I think) that Johnson had a bad ear. But we cannot accuse Dryden of that. Even Wordsworth admitted that he had 'an excellent ear'. Dryden was not speaking casually, but deliberately, and late in life after he had said more than once that Milton was one of the world's great poets. He cannot have liked Milton's attack on rhyme as 'the invention of a barbarous age to set off wretched matter and lame metre'; and indeed Milton might have given him his cue by saying that rhyme imposed on modern poets 'vexation, hindrance, and constraint to express many things otherwise, and for the most part worse, than else they would have expressed them'. Milton says that rhyme exercises a constraint in general; and Dryden says that it exercised an obvious constraint on Milton. We are left in no doubt that he could not read Milton's early poems without repeatedly thinking that the rhyming word had been sought for and did not take its place in the flow of the sense inevitably. If he noticed that there are ten un-rhymed lines in *Lycidas* he may have thought that Milton had failed to see how to rhyme them, and as they do not fall within a clear prosodic scheme, he may have looked on them as blemishes. We, of course, may think differently. But only thus, as far as I see, can we explain the statement that 'rhyme was not his talent'—which means that he did not find rhyme 'easy', that his 'unpremeditated verse' was blank verse. It is a hard saying. Difficulties of this kind serve to keep the business of criticism alive, and lively.

Dryden passed from Milton to Shakespeare to write a variation on the theme of *Antony and Cleopatra*. We sometimes hear *All for Love* spoken of as if it were an attempt to improve on Shakespeare. It was not that. It was an attempt to tell a part of the story of *Antony and Cleopatra* in a different manner. 'I have written against the Three Unities, I know that they are not necessary to a just drama, I know that they are not in the English tradition, but let me see what I can make of them': something like that Dryden said to himself. The story had been dramatized in English by others than Shakespeare—by Samuel Daniel, and Thomas May, and Sir Charles Sedley (the Lisideius of the Essay *Of Dramatick Poesy*), and their example, as Dryden tells us, gave him confidence 'to try myself in the bow of Ulysses amongst the crowd of suitors'; but he was urged on to telling it in a new manner by his reading of Racine's latest play, *Phèdre*, for which apparently he did not greatly care. He preferred Corneille to Racine. Familiar as he was with the French drama, he did not like its drawing of character. He thought that Racine had transformed the Hippolytus of Euripides into Monsieur Hippolyte. Still *Phèdre* showed how the three Unities could be used, and, as all the learned critics were saying, they had their warrant in the drama of Greece and Rome. 'Mr. Rymer', he remarks, 'has judiciously observed'—he did not always think him judicious—'that the Ancients are and ought to be our masters.' Good and well! Now for an experiment! And when *All for Love* is finished he says that 'the Unities of Time, Place, and Action [are] more exactly observed than perhaps the English theatre requires'.

It is the observance of the Unity of Time that controls the differences from Shakespeare's play in subject, and characterization, and pace, and colour. If the action is to be confined to one day, and if the play is to be a tragedy, the hero and heroine must be seen only in the last day of their lives. French critics debated the length of the day. One of them argued that as a play takes about three hours to perform, the action of an ideal play would not extend beyond three hours, as if a representation of life should proceed at the same pace as real life. This was thought to be too exacting, and twelve hours was proposed as a reasonable limit, but the general conclusion was that the time ought to be twenty-four hours with the option on rare occasions of thirty. It all seems rather absurd when put down in figures, but what is not absurd is the rule that the action ought to begin as near the catastrophe as the dramatist can contrive. The Unity of Time compelled Dryden to take only the concluding matter of Shakespeare's play—roughly what is found in the last two acts—and to expand that into a play of five acts. As a consequence there was a great reduction in the number of scenes and speaking parts—and, inevitably, a new Antony. Shakespeare's Antony must be a nobler character because we see him at the height of his power while Fortune was sometimes kind. His power is steadily sapped, yet we understand the devotion of his soldiers and the anxiety of his friends. He is ruined, and the magnificence of the ruin is impressed on us. But, because the action has to begin as near the catastrophe as is possible, we are never given the chance to admire Dryden's Antony. We see, and can see only, the Antony of the last phase, when he is the flickering ember of his glowing manhood. There was not the same reason for the inferiority of Dryden's Cleopatra. Shakespeare's is as great in death as in life, but age has begun to wither Dryden's. Passion has worn her. She has Antony in her toils, but she is in toils also, and when the end comes we are not moved as Shakespeare moves us. But Dryden's Cleopatra is well drawn, and is more within the range of ordinary experience.

All for Love is a sombre play in comparison with Shakespeare's, which is suffused with the splendour of the Mediterranean sun. Of all Shakespeare's dramas none has so bright a colouring as *Antony and Cleopatra*. I would not suggest that Dryden could have given us the same sense of light and warmth, but he had to adopt a different colour scheme—from the very beginning he had to tone his colour to the impending catastrophe because he was to tell us what happened on one tragic day, because he was conforming to the Unity of Time.

It is Dryden's best play. He knew that, with the aid of Shakespeare, he had risen above his normal level in the drama. 'I hope I may affirm, and without vanity, that by imitating him, I have excelled myself throughout the play.' He says 'imitating him', but he means following him and thinking of his example. In passages he did definitely imitate; he worked on many of Shakespeare's ideas and descriptions. But the play is not an imitation. It is a transmutation by a gifted artist who knew his powers and their limits. To call it a triumph of craftsmanship, which it certainly is, may be to suggest only a triumph in the rehandling of substance that is available in methods that are known. But Dryden used a tool of his own devising—his own blank verse. That is the great innovation in *All for Love*. Again he gives Shakespeare

the credit. 'In my style I have professed to imitate the
divine Shakespeare; which that I might perform more
freely, I have disencumbered myself from rhyme.' But
his blank verse is not Shakespeare's. He cites the passage
which he liked best, and a portion of it I must quote.
Ventidius has come to urge Antony to action, and Antony
replies—

> I know thy meaning.
> But I have lost my Reason, have disgrac'd
> The name of Soldier, with inglorious ease;
> In the full Vintage of my flowing honors,
> Sat still, and saw it prest by other hands.
> Fortune came smiling to my youth, and woo'd it,
> And purple greatness met my ripen'd years.
> When first I came to Empire, I was born
> On Tides of People, crouding to my Triumphs;
> The wish of Nations; and the willing World
> Receiv'd me as its pledge of future peace;
> I was so great, so happy, so belov'd,
> Fate could not ruine me; till I took pains
> And work'd against my Fortune, chid her from me,
> And turn'd her loose; yet still she came again.
> My careless dayes, and my luxurious nights,
> At length have weary'd her, and now she's gone,
> Gone, gone, divorc'd for ever. Help me, Soldier,
> To curse this Mad-man, this industrious Fool,
> Who labour'd to be wretched: pr'ythee curse me.

I quote this passage the more readily as so far I have
quoted only rhymed verse. Let us ask ourselves this
question—Who since Dryden has written better blank
verse in the drama?

III

SATIRES AND RELIGIOUS POEMS

I propose to speak to-day of Dryden's satires and religious poems. When he brought out his *All for Love* he
was growing weary of the drama. He had excelled himself in that play—so he said, and so we say—but he was
feeling more and more the strain of an occupation for
which he thought himself not wholly suited. He had
a higher ambition. Even before he wrote *Aureng-zebe*,
the last and the best of his rhymed plays, he had been
thinking of an epic. 'A heroic poem, truly such, is undoubtedly the greatest work which the soul of man is
capable to perform'—thus he began his essay on the
epic, where he combats the view expressed by Aristotle
at the end of the *Poetics* that tragedy is the higher art.
It was a reasonable ambition, for England lacked a
national epic; and he might have been encouraged to it
by the activity of the poets in France who, since the
middle of the century, had produced at least six epics,
in the endeavour to do for their country, and to out-do,
what Virgil had done for Rome. And France had just
produced the accepted critical treatise, the *Traité du
Poème Epique* by Le Bossu, which Dryden knew well and
treated with great respect; he calls Le Bossu 'the best
of modern critics'. The need for a great modern epic was,
we have to remember, in the background of *Paradise
Lost*. But that majestic poem had not met the national
demand, for Milton had gone beyond it in writing an epic
of mankind. Nor had *The Faerie Queene* met it, as Dryden

is careful to tell us. *The Faerie Queene* even if it had been completed 'could not have been perfect because the model was not true'—there was not sufficient unity in its design. The way was still open, and Dryden was prepared to take it, if he could. He thought of devoting the rest of his life to a poem in 'honour of my native country'. But he could not decide on the historical events on which it should be based. For a while he favoured King Arthur, as Milton had done in his young days before he turned to Adam and man's first disobedience. Before Milton, Ben Jonson had said in his conversations with Drummond of Hawthornden that 'for a Heroic poem there was no such ground as King Arthur's fiction'. But Arthur proved to be too shadowy for Dryden, who, it is not rash to say, knew nothing about the Arthurian romances, and very little about the Arthurian story. He read Bede and other Latin authors in search of information, and learned that the heathen Anglo-Saxons had strange rites and customs. The subject, as he saw it, would allow great scope for his invention; but his invention would have been sorely tried to raise on such a foundation a poem to the glory of the English people. He left the epic to be written by Sir Richard Blackmore. His own *King Arthur* was to be only a dramatic opera, which lives in the music of Purcell. Among its many songs is 'Fairest isle, all isles excelling'.

The other subject which he considered for his epic was Edward the Black Prince's campaign in Spain, and he appears to have thought it in every way suitable—more suitable, I imagine, than any of us think it. But nothing happened. He never wrote his epic, and we need not stay to consider what we have lost, though that might employ our critical faculties pleasantly in a vacant hour. Sir

Walter Scott employed his when he said that 'we should have found picturesque narrative detailed in the most manly and majestic verse, and interspersed with lessons teaching us to know human life, maxims proper to guide it, and sentiments which ought to adorn it'. We can be content with that. But of one thing we may be certain. Dryden attained to greater eminence in the work which he was to take in hand. He could not have given us our greatest epic; but he is our greatest satirist. As a political satire *Absalom and Achitophel* has no rival.

He did not begin with political satire. The prefaces which he wrote during the decade when he was the leading dramatist show that his plays met with a steady stream of fault-finding in addition to the banter contained in the good-humoured *Rehearsal*. Once he replied in kind, when he joined in a prose trouncing of Elkanah Settle who had set up as a rival in the heroic play, but in general he was content to let the attacks pass with only a reference to them in the prefaces. We get a rather unpleasant impression of the dramatic circles at this time, with their rivalries and jealousies and uneasy relations smoothed over by reconciliations which were more convenient than sincere. Such, for a time, were his relations with Shadwell. This rival in comedy, who took Ben Jonson as his model and found his subjects in the ordinary life of the time, and in so doing has provided the social historian with better material than Dryden has done—this rival sneered at the

> dull Romantick whining Play,
> Where poor frail Woman's made a Deity,
> With sensless amorous Idolatry,
> And snivelling Heroes sigh, and pine, and cry.
> Though singly they beat Armies, and huff Kings,
> Rant at the Gods, and do impossible things;

Though they can laugh at danger, bloud and wounds
Yet if the Dame once chides, the milksop Hero swoons.
These doughty things, nor Manners have, nor Wit;
We ne'r saw Hero fit to drink with yet.[1]

None the less Shadwell had got on to good terms with
Dryden—good enough at least for Dryden to provide
the prologue to one of his plays.[2] It might have been the
prologue to many another play. Still, it served as a prologue to one of Shadwell's. Then something happened,
and the time for reconciliation had passed. In the year
in which he wrote this prologue he wrote *MacFlecknoe*
to put an end to their equivocal relations, and henceforward Shadwell was to be the unforgiven butt of his
ridicule.

MacFlecknoe was written in 1678. That is the date on
the transcript in the hand of Dryden's young friend John
Oldham, now in the Bodleian Library. The date is important as it has altered what was for many years the
accepted view of Dryden's development as a satirist.
His definite satires, apart from his poems with satirical
passages, belong to a very short period, and *MacFlecknoe*
was thought to be the last of them. We now know that
it was the first. It circulated in manuscript and was
printed in 1682, apparently without Dryden's sanction,
certainly without his supervision. The first good text did
not appear till 1684, when Dryden included it anony-
mously in a volume of *Miscellany Poems*;[3] and several
more years were to pass before he acknowledged it in
his *Discourse concerning Satire*.

[1] Epilogue to *The Virtuoso* (1676).

[2] *A True Widow*, produced 21 March 1678, published 1679 (preface
dated 16 February 1678/9).

[3] In this volume *MacFlecknoe* is printed first in the group of his satires
with which the volume opens; he preserved their chronological order.

We can understand why Dryden delayed publication. It was a personal satire arising out of a private quarrel, and there was no call to publish it if it could be read in manuscript by Shadwell and the circles in which they both moved. In this respect it was like Pope's satirical portrait of Addison, which for several years was known only in manuscript but could not escape the printer, and after appearing in a journal and elsewhere was included in his *Epistle to Arbuthnot*. There is however this difference, that Pope's resentment had never wholly overcome his admiration of Addison, and he publicly acknowledged what had been a portrait of an individual only after he had converted it into a portrait of a type, whereas Dryden never found anything to admire in Shadwell and nothing in *MacFlecknoe* did he wish to alter. 'Addison' became 'Atticus', but 'Shadwell' remained 'Shadwell'. The satire is the more telling as it is all conveyed in the praises of a notoriously bad poet. Richard Flecknoe, who had occasionally tilted at Dryden and now paid the penalty of being placed on the throne of dulness, is represented as nominating his successor. He has only one possible choice:

> All humane things are subject to decay,
> And, when Fate summons, Monarchs must obey:
> This *Fleckno* found, who, like *Augustus*, young
> Was call'd to Empire, and had govern'd long:
> In Prose and Verse, was own'd, without dispute
> Through all the Realms of *Nonsense*, absolute.
> This aged Prince now flourishing in Peace,
> And blest with issue of a large increase,
> Worn out with business, did at length debate
> To settle the succession of the State:
> And pond'ring which of all his Sons was fit
> To Reign, and wage immortal War with Wit:

Cry'd, 'tis resolv'd; for Nature pleads that He
Should onely rule, who most resembles me:
Sh—— alone my perfect image bears,
Mature in dullness from his tender years;
Sh—— alone, of all my Sons, is he
Who stands confirm'd in full stupidity.
The rest to some faint meaning make pretence,
But *Sh*—— never deviates into sense.

Shadwell is transfixed in these lines, and can never escape from them. It is a brilliant opening, but it is the best part of the poem. In the speeches of Flecknoe which follow, Shadwell's incompetences, and in particular the great fault of dulness—in Flecknoe's eyes the great merit—are held up for continuous contempt, and the mockery becomes a little less amusing. But the sheer power exerted in this poem is overwhelming. English literature can show no comparable example of a poet's smothering of a rival. And the poem holds an important place in the history of our literature. Dryden prided himself on its being our first mock-heroic. A trivial subject is treated as if it were great; the setting and the style of an heroic poem are employed for the ridicule of literary incompetence. It is the direct ancestor of *The Dunciad*, but Dryden's subject was one man, and Pope's was a motley company.

His first satire to be published was *Absalom and Achitophel*. It came to the aid of the crown at a grave constitutional crisis, when the Whig party under the Earl of Shaftesbury tried to secure that Charles should be succeeded on the throne, not by his brother who was a Roman Catholic, but by his natural son, the Duke of Monmouth, who was a Protestant. He wrote it with great care; he was creating a new kind of satire.

We cannot fail to be struck with the temper of *Absalom and Achitophel*. Dryden here holds himself in perfect control, and his hardest blows betray no rancour. The temper of satire was a matter of great interest to him, as we learn from the essay which he prefixed to his translation of Juvenal. He there writes a long comparison of Juvenal with Horace and Persius, refers to the satires of Boileau, and speaks briefly about his own. He does not rank himself with the great Latin satirists, but he makes it clear that he knows where his methods differ from theirs, and that he was not unwilling to be placed in their company. Part of what he says I must quote:

The nicest and most delicate touches of Satire consist in fine Raillery. . . . How easie it is to call Rogue and Villain, and that wittily! But how hard to make a Man appear a Fool, a Blockhead, or a Knave, without using any of those opprobrious terms! . . . Neither is it true, that this fineness of Raillery is offensive. A witty Man is tickl'd while he is hurt in this manner; and a Fool feels it not. The occasion of an Offence may possibly be given, but he cannot take it. If it be granted that in effect this way does more Mischief; that a Man is secretly wounded, and though he be not sensible himself, yet the malicious World will find it for him: Yet there is still a vast difference betwixt the slovenly Butchering of a Man, and the fineness of a stroak that separates the Head from the Body, and leaves it standing in its place. A man may be capable, as *Jack Ketche*'s Wife said of his Servant, of a plain piece of Work, a bare Hanging; but to make a Malefactor die sweetly, was only belonging to her Husband. I wish I cou'd apply it to my self, if the Reader wou'd be kind enough to think it belongs to me. The Character of *Zimri* in my *Absalom* is, in my Opinion, worth the whole Poem: 'Tis not bloody, but 'tis ridiculous enough. And he for whom it was intended, was too witty to resent it as an injury. If I had rail'd, I might have suffer'd for it justly: But I manag'd my own Work more happily, perhaps more dextrously. I avoided the mention of great Crimes, and apply'd my self to the representing of Blind-sides, and little Extravagancies: To which, the wittier a Man is, he is generally the more obnoxious. It succeeded as I wish'd; the Jest went round, and he was laught at in his turn who began the Frolick.

(Which of course is a reference to *The Rehearsal*, for Zimri represents the Duke of Buckingham.)

It is easy to rail. There had been plenty of railing in earlier English satire. But railing is one thing, and fine raillery is another. 'Satire', he says in the same essay, 'is a poem of a difficult nature in itself, and is not written to vulgar readers.'

Many of us, I think, will confess to some surprise at Dryden's statement that he thought the character sketch of Zimri worth the whole poem. Certainly his fine raillery is nowhere seen to better advantage than in this picture of

> A man so various, that he seem'd to be
> Not one, but all Mankind's Epitome.
> Stiff in Opinions, always in the wrong;
> Was every thing by starts, and nothing long....
> Rayling and praising were his usual Theams,
> And both (to shew his Judgment) in Extreams....
> In squandring Wealth was his peculiar Art,
> Nothing went unrewarded, but Desert.

A satirical portrait must be in some respects a caricature, but a good caricature is a likeness. Dryden knew that he had represented the Duke of Buckingham unmistakably, and no doubt he liked the portrait the better as it paid off an old score. But it is difficult to believe that he could have underestimated the character sketch which is the pivot of the poem. Achitophel is the villain of the piece, 'for close designs and crooked counsels fit', but he has to

51

be represented as a man of very great capacity, of capacity that has been misapplied. We need not inquire how far Achitophel is a credible portrait of the Earl of Shaftesbury. That is a matter for the historian. But Achitophel is certainly a credible portrait of a dangerous politician who has won his way to great power and in the eyes of his opponents appears to be 'resolved to ruin or to rule the state'. He must have his merits:

> A daring Pilot in extremity,
> Pleas'd with the Danger, when the Waves went high
> He sought the Storms; but for a Calm unfit,
> Would Steer too nigh the Sands, to boast his Wit.
> Great Wits are sure to Madness near ally'd,
> And thin Partitions do their Bounds divide.

Only if the merits were admitted would the portrait become credible; and when they were admitted, the crime of their misapplication would appear the greater. So much importance did Dryden attach to this element of praise that he added to it in the second edition of the poem—unless it be that a little passage had been inadvertently omitted in the first, and the neatness with which it joins on to the succeeding lines gives strong support to this conjecture. (Unfortunately we do not have a single original manuscript of any one of Dryden's poems to help us in our textual problems.) Shaftesbury had been a good Lord Chancellor, and part of the added, or omitted, passage is this—

> Yet, Fame deserv'd, no Enemy can grudge;
> The Statesman we abhor, but praise the Judge.
> In *Israel*'s Courts ne'er sat an *Abbethdin*
> With more discerning Eyes, or Hands more clean:
> Unbrib'd, unsought, the Wretched to redress;
> Swift of Dispatch, and easie of Access.

I confess I do not know why Dryden preferred his Zimri to his Achitophel—why he said that his Zimri was worth the whole poem, which it certainly is not, though one is bold in contradicting flatly anything that Dryden said about his own work. Perhaps he only meant as good as anything in the poem. The Zimri is neater than the Achitophel. It is a self-contained little unit which says all that Dryden wanted to say. It might all have been in his mind before he began to write it. But he might not have foreseen what shape all his Achitophel was to take. It develops as the story proceeds, and for this reason we feel it to be more alive than the Zimri, which is comparatively static. But there is no call for a comparison. Achitophel controls the action of the poem, whereas Zimri does not—he is in fact described and done with,

> For, spight of him, the weight of Business fell
> On *Absalom* and wise *Achitophel.*

Dryden had to be discreet in drawing Absalom, for he had enjoyed Monmouth's favour and in a greater degree the esteem and patronage of the Duchess, and Charles had a natural liking for his handsome and attractive son. So the line which he took was to be kind to him and to represent him as Shaftesbury's dupe:

> 'Tis Juster to Lament him, than Accuse.

His temptation and fall are meant to remind us of *Paradise Lost*—

> Him Staggering so when Hell's dire Agent found,
> While fainting Vertue scarce maintain'd her Ground,
> He pours fresh Forces in.

There are no severer lines in the whole poem. This is not the gentle treatment of fine raillery, nor was it extended

to all the members of Shaftesbury's party. Sir Slingsby
Bethel and Titus Oates are drawn so contemptuously as
to be almost comic characters. In contrast, we have the
portraits of Charles's friends, none of whom is better
drawn than the Marquess of Halifax—the Trimmer as
he was soon to be called, and as he was pleased to call
himself because he aimed at trimming the political boat.
It is a brief sketch, but it has the interest of anticipating
this title, and anticipating the reputation in which he is
now generally held; and it is not the only portrait of
which this may be said:

> *Jotham* of piercing Wit and pregnant Thought:
> Endew'd by Nature, and by Learning taught
> To move Assemblies, who but onely tri'd
> The worse awhile, then chose the better side;
> Nor chose alone, but turn'd the Balance too;
> So much the weight of one brave man can do.

Absalom and Achitophel is a portrait gallery of the leading
politicians at the time of the Exclusion Bill. Fools and
rogues predominate. They must, for the poem is a satire.
But the gallery in this satire is one of the great galleries
in English literature.

Dryden put the best of his skill in character drawing
into *Absalom and Achitophel*. His dramas had shown
weakness in characterization, as he admitted. When he
drew types he had difficulty in turning them into re-
cognizable persons. But in this poem he had to begin
with the individual. If Achitophel becomes a portrait of
a crafty, crooked, self-seeking politician, he still remains
an individual, and as an individual we remember him.
Omit details, and the politicians in *Absalom and Achitophel*
might be politicians of other times. Study of the
historical background will enable us to see the poem as

a contribution to a controversy, but Dryden raises the poem high above the circumstances from which it sprang, otherwise we should not be thinking of it now.

Not only in character drawing did Dryden give to satire the best of his skill. He gave it also in his verse. Hitherto English satire had been rough, even purposely rough, as if the ruder the weapon the uglier would be the wound. Apart from Butler, the leading satirist since the Restoration had been Andrew Marvell. Butler had looked back to Commonwealth times in *Hudibras*, and with a sense of escape from a dreary domination had spun verse after verse in mockery of its agents and what they stood for, and though his poem took on at times the wider interest of a satire on the follies of human nature, his mind was centred in events and conditions that had passed. But Marvell's satires were inspired by his anxiety at the way things had been going since the Restoration. If we did not know for certain that they are his, we should hesitate to attribute them to the delicate poet of *The Garden* and the *Coy Mistress* whom we associate with 'a green thought in a green shade', who reminds us that

> At my back I always hear
> Time's winged chariot hurrying near.

In his satires Marvell abandons all semblance of this delicacy; he speaks his mind bluntly and he writes roughly. Clearly he thought that satire need not be, perhaps should not be, written otherwise.

The prominent satirist immediately before Dryden, while the agitation over the Exclusion Bill was coming to a height, was John Oldham, the young friend who by his *Satyrs upon the Jesuits* was to win the praise of having been a forerunner to the same goal. I have had occasion to quote from the poem which Dryden wrote on Oldham's early death, where it is said that advancing age would have taught him the numbers of his native tongue. But what does it matter, Dryden adds, that he was still learning them?

> But Satire needs not these, and Wit will shine
> Through the harsh cadence of a rugged line.

Satire to be effective does not require a command of versification, he admits, remembering the other English satirists. But he was long past the stage of asking his own wit 'to shine through the harsh cadence of a rugged line'. When he turned to satire, he had achieved such a mastery of the couplet, that he could not go back on his training—and this training, let it be remembered, had been given him by the rhymed drama. Let those write rough verses who cannot do better, but let those who can write well employ their art to make satire more telling. Why should satire be distinguished by rough manners and careless speech? Whatever it may say, let it cultivate the graces. Henceforward satire was not to revert to its cruder habits. Dryden set a standard for his successors. He raised English satire to the rank of an art.

The subject and design of the poem are said to have been suggested by the king. Old Testament analogies were common in political writings at this time, and the analogy on which Dryden bases his poem had occurred to many before him; but there is no reason for not accepting the story that Charles asked his poet laureate to turn the analogy to account in his service. For *Absalom and Achitophel* is an official poem, designed as a weapon in a very bitter fight. It is unmistakably official in its conclusion, which gives a rendering not—as has often been stated—of Charles's speech on opening the Oxford parliament, but—as has recently been shown—of what Charles had stated in a public *Declaration*.[1] And it is more than likely that Dryden had told Charles how he proposed to begin the poem, and that Charles made no objection, perhaps was amused. An official poem, it is a laureate poem, the first poem that Dryden published as poet laureate. In its temper, and its character sketches, and its structure, and its verse, it embodied a new conception of satire. We are apt to associate the laureateship only with odes and decorative effusions, but it gave us the art of satire; and that is the greatest gift of the laureateship to English literature.

'They who can criticize so weakly as to imagine I have done my worst', he said, 'may be convinced at their own cost that I can write severely with more ease than I can gently.' He soon found occasion to write more severely— but not better. When the attempted prosecution of Shaftesbury failed, his party struck a medal in his honour; and again the king is said to have asked for a poem. The story goes that 'One day as the King was walking in the Mall and talking with Dryden, he said, "If I was a poet, and I think I am poor enough to be one, I would write a poem on such a subject in the following manner"'. Whatever the truth of this story, Dryden's next poem was *The Medal*. It resumes the attack on Shaftesbury, but the blows are not so cleverly delivered. He was not in the same mood to play, and he cannot have written this poem with so much pleasure. The growing

---

[1] See 'The Conclusion of Dryden's *Absalom and Achitophel*', by Godfrey Davies, *The Huntington Library Quarterly*, x, i (November 1946), p. 69.

seriousness of the political situation compelled him to think not only of the stages by which Shaftesbury had risen to power and of his methods of exerting it, as in *Absalom and Achitophel*, but of the consequences that would follow if this 'Pander of the people's hearts' were to succeed in his designs. The instability of the 'Almighty Crowd' comes in for pungent exposure. But Dryden finds reassurance in the latent sanity of the English political temperament.

> Such impious Axiomes foolishly they show;
> For in some Soyles Republiques will not grow:
> Our Temp'rate Isle will no extremes sustain,
> Of pop'lar Sway, or Arbitrary Reign:
> But slides between them both into the best;
> Secure in Freedom, in a Monarch blest.
> And though the Clymate, vex't with various Winds,
> Works through our yielding Bodies, on our Minds,
> The wholsome Tempest purges what it breeds,
> To recommend the Calmness that succeeds.

This poem, better than *Absalom and Achitophel*, shows where Dryden himself stood politically. His sympathies were with the established order, but he was not an out-and-out party man. In a prose pamphlet written about this time, after remarking that in the previous year he had spoken to only four men of the opposite party, he continues—

We have been acquaintence of a long standing, many years before this accursed Plot divided men into several Parties: I dare call them to witness, whether the most I have at any time said, will amount to more than this, that *I hop'd the time would come when these names of* Whig *and* Tory *would cease among us; and that we might live together, as we had done formerly* . . . they have severally own'd to me, that all men who espouse a Party, must expect to be blacken'd by the contrary Side.[1]

He was glad to be done with his laureate satires. When a second part of *Absalom and Achitophel* was called for, he was content to supply only a section of it, and that section dealt not with politicians but with political writers, among them Elkanah Settle and Shadwell. He returned to literary satire, and to personal satire. Doeg and Og, as he names them, are

> Two Fools that Crutch their Feeble sense on Verse;
> Who by my Muse, to all succeeding times,
> Shall live in spight of their own Dogrell Rhimes.

The prophecy made with such boisterous confidence has been largely fulfilled. Settle and Shadwell both owe a great part of their reputation to Dryden. Settle is represented only as an incompetent writer. He had answered *Absalom and Achitophel* in verse that was a lame imitation of Dryden's, but Dryden did not forget his heroic plays.

> *Doeg*, though without knowing how or why,
> Made still a blund'ring kind of Melody; . . .
> He was too warm on Picking-work to dwell,
> But Faggotted his Notions as they fell,
> And if they Rhim'd and Rattl'd all was well.

But this is gentler treatment than what is meted out to Shadwell, for Dryden took him to be, and probably rightly, the author of the scurrilous reply to *The Medal* called *The Medal of John Bayes*, in which gossip and scandal make up an account of Dryden's past life. This account explains Dryden's couplet

> I will not rake the Dunghill of thy Crimes,
> For who woud read thy Life that reads thy Rhimes?

[1] *The Vindication . . . The Duke of Guise* (1683), p. 21.

He will not rake up the past—he has more than enough
in Shadwell as he is:

> With all this Bulk there's nothing lost in *Og*,
> For ev'ry inch that is not Fool is Rogue.

The whole passage vibrates with contempt; it suggests
even physical aversion. Within a month of its publication,
MacFlecknoe appeared for the first time in print, though
the authorized text (as we have seen) did not appear till
a little later. Dryden's relations with Shadwell do not
make a pleasant story. But by this time he was thinking
of something better.

The transition from the satires to the *Religio Laici*
was not so violent as may at first appear. He had been
engaged on this serious poem while he was still writing
his satires, and they overlap in more than time. In *The
Medal*, for instance, when speaking of the factious religious sects which

> rack ev'n Scripture to confess their Cause,
> And plead a Call to preach, in spight of Laws,

he had said

> But, since our Sects in prophecy grow higher,
> The Text inspires not them, but they the Text inspire.

This couplet might have been in the passage on the Non-
conformists in *Religio Laici*. But we can go much further
back. We have seen how he was preoccupied with questions of Fate, and Faith, and Reason in his heroic plays.
We have seen too that even his Essay *Of Dramatick
Poesie* is evidence, as he wished it to be, of his sceptical
turn of mind, and that he wrote this Essay to clear up
some of his doubts by putting them on paper. He now
writes the *Religio Laici* to make sure as well as he can

where he stands as a churchman. The poem was wholly spontaneous. He assumes 'an honest layman's liberty', and argues out his problems for the peace of his own mind. It is an eminently sincere poem. His other work to which it has most resemblance in method and spirit is the *Dramatick Poesie*, where conflicting views are balanced fairly. But in *Religio Laici* a decision is come to, and we are provided with a good statement for the *via media* of the Church of England. That Dryden was to find in the course of a few years that the *via media* did not satisfy him does not matter—that does not affect the clearness of the argument, and the excellence of the verse. He calls it 'unpolished rugged verse' because of its colloquial quality, but none of us will call it rugged. There may be less imagery than is usual. 'The expressions of a poem designed purely for instruction', he says, 'ought to be plain and natural, and yet majestic.' Plain and natural expressions, but not rugged verse. There is the perfection of modulated verse in the magnificent opening; and here, too, there is majesty, and imagery which he never excelled.

> Dim as the borrow'd beams of Moon and Stars
> To *lonely, weary, wandring* Travellers,
> Is *Reason* to the *Soul*: and as on high
> Those rowling Fires *discover* but the Sky,
> Not light us *here*; So *Reason's* glimmering Ray
> Was lent, not to *assure* our *doubtfull* way,
> But *guide* us upward to a *better* Day.
> And as those nightly Tapers disappear
> When Day's bright Lord ascends our Hemisphere,
> So pale grows *Reason* at *Religions* sight,
> So *dyes*, and so *dissolves* in *Supernatural Light*.

The weakness of human reason was a common theme in what we choose to keep on calling the Age of Reason—

and why we do so, not many of us stay to consider. We hear very much less about the weakness of human reason nowadays.

The title is sometimes thought to have been suggested by Sir Thomas Browne's *Religio Medici*. It might quite as well have been suggested by the *Religio Stoici* (1665) of Sir George Mackenzie, whom Dryden had known for some time. In the preface to his translation of Juvenal (1693) he speaks of a conversation which he had on poetry 'about twenty years ago' with 'that noble wit of Scotland, Sir George Mackenzie'. But it was the right title for a poem on the religious difficulties of an 'honest layman'.

Religio Laici is the poem of a doubter who is anxious to believe, and is so far from conviction that he will listen to the call of expediency. I would draw your attention to the lines at the conclusion:

> And, after hearing what our Church can say,
> If still our Reason runs another way,
> That private Reason 'tis more Just to curb
> Than by Disputes the publick Peace disturb.
> For points obscure are of small use to learn,
> But *Common quiet* is *Mankind's concern*.

The public peace has no bearing on private doubts. One way or another the poem contains clear evidence that though Dryden had argued himself to a decision he had not reached a resting place. This he found a year or two later, on the accession of James II, when he became a Roman Catholic. Quite a good case can be made for the view that he would have remained much as he was under Charles if James had been a Protestant. But we must not forget that he had been steadily moving from scepticism to a settled belief and had been troubled, as the *Religio Laici* shows us, by the fallibility of private judgement.

On this question no one, as far as I am aware, has written with greater understanding and sympathy than Sir Walter Scott. But our concern now is with the poem in which Dryden defended his new faith—*The Hind and the Panther*.

It is by far the longest of his original poems, but it is a strange poem, and it leaves many of its readers in doubt what to think of it. It is disappointing in its structure; as he himself would seem to have suspected when he explained in the preface the relation and purpose of the three Parts. A poem that is mainly an argument could not be expected to possess the dramatic quality of *Absalom and Achitophel*, but we have still to say that the outlines are not so clearly drawn as in the less ambitious *Religio Laici*. And the poem suffers from not ending as Dryden had intended. He tells us that 'it was neither imposed on me nor so much as the subject given me by any man'. None the less it is an unofficial laureate poem, written not merely in defence of his new religion but also in support of the policy of James. He had begun it while James still hoped that the Church of England would ally itself with the Roman Catholics against the Dissenters, but when James found that he could not secure for the Roman Catholics the freedom which he meant to refuse to the Dissenters he changed his policy and aimed at an alliance with the Dissenters against the Church of England by promising freedom to all. 'About a fortnight before I had finished it', Dryden tells us, 'his Majesty's declaration for Liberty of Conscience came abroad; which if I had so expected, I might have spared myself the labour of writing many things which are contained in the Third Part of it. But I was always in some hope that the Church of England might have been persuaded to have taken off the Penal Laws and the Test, which was one design of the Poem when I proposed to myself the writing of it'. As a consequence of the change in the royal policy, Dryden, in this fortnight, changed his attitude to the Church of England. He aimed his satire at it, whereas he had begun by treating it with some tenderness. The Panther was a spotted beast, but it was 'the fairest creature of the spotted kind'; it was even 'the lady of the spotted muff'.

The first question which we are likely to ask on reading this poem is, why did Dryden revert to the old beast allegory? What could be gained by calling the Church of England the Panther and introducing a motley collection of other beasts? We always expect the Fox to be cunning, but we do not assign intellectual or moral qualities to many beasts, and Dryden's have no obvious aptness for the role which he gives them. The Bear, and the Boar, and the Wolf—for what part in a religious allegory is any one of them better suited than the others? They might have exchanged their names without any inconvenience. Dryden anticipates the objection to his beasts:

> Much malice mingl'd with a little wit
> Perhaps may censure this mysterious writ,
> Because the Muse has peopl'd *Caledon*
> With *Panthers*, *Bears*, and *Wolves*, and Beasts unknown.

There need not be any malice in the censure. The Hind is innocent, and gentle, and guileless, but this simple and beautiful creature is encumbered in a very heavy coil of argumentation. Dryden does not meet the objection by citing Aesop and Spenser's *Mother Hubberd's Tale*. This is an elaborate poem. He may have thought that the beasts would lighten it and make it more attractive to the ordinary reader, but he could not overcome the inevitable incongruity.

But the poem is Dryden's, and that means that there are many memorable passages in it, and these make the fortune of the poem. They range from sayings which have only to be read to be remembered, to the story of the swallows—a distinct story of itself, as he said—which shows closer observation of country life than is commonly credited to him, and a command of vivid, rapid narrative which he might have shown in his Epic and was yet to show at its best in his Fables. One passage is definitely autobiographical—

> My thoughtless youth was wing'd with vain desires,
> My manhood, long misled by wandring fires,
> Follow'd false lights; and when their glimps was gone,
> My pride struck out new sparkles of her own.
> Such was I, such by nature still I am.

And in another he is thinking of himself, when the Hind counsels 'a long farewell to worldly fame'—

> And what thou didst, and do'st so dearly prize,
> That fame, that darling fame, make that thy sacrifice.

Simple sincerity and calculated satire, description and argument, are curiously mingled in this poem, which leaves the reader admiring the power and the technical mastery in every page of it, but not, as I have suggested, with a clear, unified impression.

Before I pass from it I must quote the opening lines, if only as an example of the characteristic modulation of his heroic couplets, now that he was a master of the numbers of his native tongue. You will note how the sense is never impeded by the structure of the verse, how the rhyme adds to the richness of the effect without in any way controlling the meaning, how the lines vary in their melody,

how even in the brief mention of the chase the ten mono-
syllables echo the thud of the hoof of the horse:

> A milk-white *Hind*, immortal and unchang'd,
> Fed on the lawns, and in the forest rang'd;
> Without unspotted, innocent within,
> She fear'd no danger, for she knew no sin.
> Yet had she oft been chas'd with horns and hounds,
> And Scythian shafts; and many winged wounds
> Aim'd at Her heart; was often forc'd to fly,
> And doom'd to death, though fated not to dy.

Admirable verse! But I have a double purpose in quoting
this passage, for it illustrates another feature of his art.
He is one of our great masters of the opening. Let us go
back and think of the beginning of the Essay *Of Dramatick
Poesie*, or *Absalom and Achitophel*, or *MacFlecknoe*, or
Religio Laici; or let us go forward to one of his very last
poems, which begins thus—

> Old as I am, for Ladies Love unfit,
> The Pow'r of Beauty I remember yet,
> Which once inflam'd my Soul, and still inspires my Wit.

Who having read this, or any of these openings, would
not read more?

IV

TRANSLATIONS, ODES, FABLES

With the abdication of James II, Dryden ceased to be
Poet Laureate and Historiographer Royal, and was
doomed to a long struggle with poverty. Lines which he
had written in *The Hind and the Panther* took on a fuller
meaning—

> Now for my converts, . . .
> Judge not by hear-say, but observe at least,
> If since their change, their loaves have been increast.

He had good patrons who had encouraged him in better
days and now helped him generously, notably the Earl
of Dorset (the Eugenius of the Essay *Of Dramatick
Poesie*), but he had to make his livelihood as best he could.
He returned to the drama and wrote five plays, with
varying success. But as a member of a penalized body,
for he never faltered in his new faith, he ceased to find his
themes in what was happening around him. He found
them rather in his reading. The great occupation of these
years was translation.

The best picture that we have of him then is given by
himself at the conclusion of his translation of Virgil—

> What *Virgil* wrote in the vigour of his Age, in Plenty and at
> Ease, I have undertaken to *Translate* in my Declining Years:
> strugling with Wants, oppress'd with Sickness, curb'd in my
> Genius, lyable to be misconstrued in all I write; and my Judges,
> if they are not very equitable, already prejudic'd against me,
> by the *Lying Character* which has been given them of my
> Morals. Yet steady to my Principles, and not dispirited with

67

my Afflictions, I have, by the Blessing of God on my Endeavours, overcome all Difficulties; and, in some measure,
acquitted my self of the Debt which I ow'd the Publick, when
I undertook this Work.

The publisher, Jacob Tonson, planned that the handsome
Folio should be dedicated to King William, but he
reckoned without Dryden, who would not be bribed into
appearing to be a supporter of the government; he would
write neither for it nor against it.

The first translations that he had published were from
Ovid; and he continued to translate from Ovid, now and
again, till the end of his life. As these translations are
scattered in various collections, it may come as a surprise
to us that they run to over 7000 lines. No Latin author
put less strain on him. He seems to have found even re-
laxation in his 5000 lines from the *Metamorphoses*. It was
Ovid, more than any other writer, who encouraged him
in his change from argumentation to narrative. But for
his long experience in translating Ovid, he might not
have written the original tales which he published in the
last year of his life. There was much that he did not
render—he was out of sympathy with what he calls Ovid's
'boyisms'—but he liked these translations. 'They appear
to me', he says of some of them, 'the best of all my
endeavours in this kind. Perhaps this poet is more easy
to be translated than some others whom I have lately
attempted; perhaps too, he was more according to my
genius.'

He would not say that Juvenal was according to his
genius, and he called in several colleagues—among them
Congreve and Creech—when asked to undertake a complete translation, and kept only five of the sixteen satires
for himself. In his own satires he was, as we have seen,

essentially a fighter, whether with an individual or for a party. However deeply he might be moved, stern denunciation was not *his* bent; indignation did not make *his* verses. Now if we take his translation of the tenth satire of Juvenal—the satire which Johnson imitated in *The Vanity of Human Wishes*—I do not think that we can help feeling that it is largely a surface translation, that its deeper significance has not been adequately conveyed. But having mentioned Johnson I must quote what he says of the work of Dryden and his collaborators as a whole: Juvenal's 'grandeur none of the hand seemed to consider as necessary to be imitated, except Creech. ...It is therefore perhaps possible to give a better representation of that great satirist, even in those parts which Dryden himself has translated, some passages excepted, which will never be excelled.' We must think that one of the passages which he had in mind was at the beginning of the tenth satire, where his own imitation had been cumbrous. Unlike Dryden, Johnson was never at his best in his openings, whether in his poems or his essays. He said—

> Let observation with extensive view
> Survey mankind, from China to Peru;
> Remark each anxious toil, each eager strife, *etc.*

We have to bend our minds to what Johnson is saying. But Dryden wins and holds us at once, in another of his great openings—

> Look round the Habitable World, how few
> Know their own Good; or knowing it, pursue.
> How void of Reason are our Hopes and Fears!
> What in the Conduct of our Life appears
> So well design'd, so luckily begun,
> But, when we have our wish, we wish undone?

Si sic omnia dixisset.

69

He was engaged on his Virgil for three years, by far
the longest time that he ever gave to a single work, and
he devoted himself to it with little interruption. His
earlier experiments with passages in the *Aeneid* had made
him fully aware of the difficulties of his task. On pub-
lishing them he had said 'they who have called Virgil the
torture of grammarians, might also have called him the
plague of translators, for he seems to have studied not to be
translated', and that 'being so very sparing of his words,
and leaving so much to be imagined by the reader, he can
never be translated as he ought, in any modern tongue'.
Further, he came to doubt if his temperament fitted him
to translate Virgil. He was convinced that he was better
fitted to translate Homer, when, after finishing his Virgil,
he turned to the first book of the *Iliad*. He then said, in
a letter, 'I find him a poet more according to my genius
than Virgil, and consequently hope I may do him
more justice in his fiery way of writing; which, as it is
liable to more faults, so it is capable of more beauties than
the exactness and sobriety of Virgil.'

Dryden's Virgil is not Virgilian, if only because he has
infused his own spirit into it. We are driven onwards by
a strong motive power, as indeed we generally are whatever he wrote. He does not invite us to linger over the
diction, over words which 'leave so much to be imagined
by the reader'. He admitted that he could not give 'in
my coarse English the thoughts and beautiful expressions
of this inimitable poet'. None the less he claimed that
he was 'the first Englishman, perhaps, who made it his
design to copy Virgil in his numbers, his choice of words,
and his placing them for the sweetness of the sound'.
I do not know that this claim can be challenged. He may
not have been the first Englishman to learn a lesson in the

mere music of verse from Virgil; but he is the first, I believe, to speak definitely of the lesson to be learned in the ordering of the vowels and the consonants. 'I must acknowledge', he says, 'that Virgil in Latin and Spenser in English have been my masters.' In his younger days he had spoken of his debt to the English poets who had immediately preceded him, such as Waller and Denham. But, looking back on his whole career towards the end of his life, he found that the two poets who had the most to tell him about the craft of verse were Spenser and Virgil. It is an important admission, to which enough attention has not yet been paid.

With all his care for his verse, he could not give us the 'atmosphere' of Virgil. A breeze blows over his pages. As Johnson said when comparing this translation with the later translation by Christopher Pitt, we read with a 'hurry of delight'. Pope, who studied it carefully, called it 'the most noble and spirited translation I know in any language'. No comparable translation of Virgil had yet appeared in English. Its only possible rival was the Scottish version, with a strong Scottish infusion, by Gavin Douglas, and neither Dryden nor Pope appears to have known it.

A 'spirited translation'. But that is not what the classical scholar expects; and the classical scholar who commends Dryden's Virgil, or Pope's Homer, is not easily found. 'A very pretty poem but not Homer', the great Bentley is reported to have said. But Dryden's Virgil and Pope's Homer are both great English poems. We must consider Dryden's aim. A translator owes a double allegiance, and he is a rare man who in a poem of any length can adjust the balance between his care for his author and his care for his own speech. In endeavouring to serve two masters he is to be expected to love one more than the other; and which he will love more will depend largely on the reader whom he has in view. Accuracy, even elegant accuracy, does not win the general reader. What is the poetical translation with which the English public nowadays is most familiar? Probably Fitzgerald's *Rubáiyát* of Omar Khayyám; and we all know that a Persian would find much in it that is new to him. Dryden had no need to think of taking so great liberties as Fitzgerald did, but he aimed at producing a translation which his contemporaries could read as a poem. He made little omissions, and little additions. 'Yet the omissions, I hope, are but of circumstances', he says; 'and the additions, I also hope, are easily deduced from Virgil's sense.' Once at least he was betrayed into a naughty little political allusion, when, to use the language of the crib, 'those who had hated their brothers during their life-time or struck their parents' was converted into

> Then they, who Brothers better Claim disown;
> Expel their Parents, and usurp the Throne.[1]

But, more important than taking liberties of that kind, he instilled a new spirit, as he knew, and could not avoid.

He gave much thought to the art of translation, and wrote about it frequently. His friend the Earl of Roscommon wrote a poem about it, *An Essay on Translated Verse*. Since the time of the Elizabethans, prose translation had given no cause for concern, but there were still no comparable translations of the great poems of antiquity. The best that Dryden knew were Chapman's Homer and Sandys's Ovid, and of neither did he think

---

[1] Ed. 1697, p. 437, (Book vi, l. 825). Pointed out by John Carey in his edition of Dryden's *Virgil* (ed. 1819), vol. i, p. xlix.

highly. Methods varied from the line-by-line rendering practised by Ben Jonson to the licence of imitation introduced by Cowley. When the need of adequate or representative translations was felt to an extent which cannot easily be appreciated by us, discussion of methods and aim was inevitable, and in this discussion, as we might expect, Dryden took a leading part. But his contribution to the theory of translation goes back, whether admittedly or indirectly, to a remark made by Sir John Denham in his preface to his translation of the second book of the *Aeneid*:

> It is not [the poet's] business alone to translate Language into Language, but Poesie into Poesie; and Poesie is of so subtile a spirit, that in pouring out of one Language into another, it will all evaporate; and if a new spirit be not added in the transfusion, there will remain nothing but a *Caput mortuum*, there being certain Graces and Happinesses peculiar to every Language, which gives life and energy to the words.

Dryden held that only if he added a new spirit could his translation become alive. Let us admit that the new spirit was liker Dryden than Virgil. But his first and greatest allegiance was to the English language, and to English verse, and in that he never wavered. 'I have endeavoured', he says, 'to make Virgil speak such English as he would himself have spoken if he had been born in England, and in this present age.' And he said much the same about his translation of Juvenal.

About the time of his early translations from Ovid and Virgil, he translated four odes of Horace, all very freely. One of these free renderings demands attention as perhaps his best illustration of the infusion of a new spirit, and not on that ground alone. It inaugurates an important development in his art. It heralds his Odes.

The title of this translation of Horace's twenty-ninth ode of his third book contains these words 'Paraphras'd in Pindarique Verse'. For the mixed blessing of this kind of verse English poetry was indebted to Abraham Cowley. He began by translating two of Pindar's odes without paying any attention to their intricate structure, even as if he had not seen that the different sections correspond in form and are all held in balance. His aim was to let the reader know what he took to be Pindar's 'way and manner of speaking', and this he thought he could do best in stanzas of any shape and lines of any length. Then he wrote original odes in the same style; and they set a new fashion for English poetry. Here was liberty for the poet who felt the constraint of the couplet. Here, too, was an invitation to slovenly writing; and there are not many Pindaric poems that we wish to read a second time, or that we can read even once. But here, too, were opportunities for poets who were capable of taking them. Let me suggest that Wordsworth's *Ode on the Intimations of Immortality* would have been called a Pindaric ode if it had been written a hundred years earlier. It is irregular in structure, the stanzas have no predetermined shape—and no one would wish that they had.

We have two kinds of Pindaric ode in English. The one corresponds in structure to Pindar's odes. Ben Jonson, who knew Greek, gave us an original poem of this kind and called it Pindaric; if Cowley had read it, he passed it by. Congreve gave us another. Gray gave us his *Bard* and *Progress of Poesy*. His letters show him counting the lines in one of the sections. This kind of Pindaric is rare in English; it is a scholar's pastime, and it forces its form on our attention. But in the other kind of Pindaric, which was far from rare in the seventeenth and eighteenth centuries, the form exercises no control, and he was a good poet who did not suffer from his unchartered freedom. He did not even tie himself to stanzas of definite form as Keats did in his greatest odes. Pindaric verse as generally understood in Dryden's time was a go-as-you-please kind of verse, and it justified itself only by its fitness to the subject-matter. Granted that the poet had something to say worth saying, the success of his poem depended on the relation of the verse rhythms to the thought. And now let me quote a part of Dryden's Pindaric paraphrase of Horace, and let us ask ourselves if the thought and the verse are in full correspondence:

> Enjoy the present smiling hour;
> And put it out of Fortune's pow'r;
> The tide of bus'ness, like the running stream,
> Is sometimes high, and sometimes low,
> A quiet ebb, or a tempestuous flow,
> And always in extream.
> Now with a noiselss gentle course
> It keeps within the middle Bed;
> Anon it lifts aloft the head,
> And bears down all before it, with impetuous force.
> And trunks of Trees come rowling down,
> Sheep and their Folds together drown:
> Both House and Homested into Seas are borne,
> And Rocks are from their old foundations torn,
> And woods made thin with winds, their scatter'd
> honours mourn.
>
> Happy the Man, and happy he alone,
> He, who can call to day his own:
> He, who secure within, can say
> Tomorrow do thy worst, for I have liv'd to day.

Be fair, or foul, or rain, or shine,
The joys I have possest, in spight of fate are mine:
Not Heav'n it self upon the past has pow'r;
But what has been, has been, and I have had my hour.

Fortune, that with malicious joy,
Does Man her slave oppress,
Proud of her Office to destroy,
Is seldome pleas'd to bless.
Still various and unconstant still;
But with an inclination to be ill;
Promotes, degrades, delights in strife,
And makes a Lottery of life.
I can enjoy her while she's kind;
But when she dances in the wind,
And shakes her wings, and will not stay,
I puff the Prostitute away:
The little or the much she gave, is quietly resign'd:
Content with poverty, my Soul I arm;
And Vertue, tho' in rags, will keep me warm.

This is far from the manner of Horace, as Dryden meant it to be. The Pindaric style gave him liberty to expand ideas which Horace had expressed without the waste of a word, and to instil a new spirit. The subject was so congenial that what began as a paraphrase became an original poem. When we ask if Dryden could have said better what he wanted to say, and if the verse contributes to the full expression of the thought, there can be only one answer.

This paraphrase was written in 1684. Having experimented so successfully with Pindaric verse he employed it in *Threnodia Augustalis*, on the death of Charles II and the accession of James—his first and his only laureate ode. It is an interesting poem, particularly in its account of Charles and Charles's reign, but most of us, I think, read it with more interest than admiration, for the subject-matter is hardly fused into unity (and if any kind of poem demands organic unity, it is the ode), and though it could have been written only by Dryden, I doubt if there is any passage in which, to use his words on another occasion, he 'excelled himself'. We may be reminded of another saying of his that verse (by which he meant the couplet) circumscribes a quick and luxuriant fancy. I cannot but think that *Threnodia Augustalis* would have been a better poem had it been shorter. But in saying this I must repeat that only Dryden could have written it.

He had now adopted Pindaric verse, and in the same year he gave another great example of it in his ode, *To the Pious Memory of Mrs. Anne Killigrew, excellent in the two Sister-Arts of Poesie and Painting*; it was prefixed to an edition of her poems. The opening stanza—yet another great opening!—sounds like the music of an organ, with its sustained swell through one long sentence. It struck the note for the whole poem; it ensured the elevation of the succeeding stanzas. There is greater unity than in the *Threnodia Augustalis*, though again there is considerable variety in the matter. The childlike innocence of her whom he is lamenting compels an apostrophe on the depravity in contemporary poetry and drama, and on his own lapses:

> O Gracious God! How far have we
> Prophan'd thy Heav'nly Gift of Poesy?
> Made prostitute and profligate the Muse,
> Debas'd to each obscene and impious use,
> Whose Harmony was first ordain'd Above
> For Tongues of Angels, and for Hymns of Love?

That was written while Dryden was about to join the Roman Catholic Church, and a good dozen years before

Jeremy Collier brought out his *Short View of the Immorality of the English Stage*. A passage of a very different kind describes the pictures which this vestal had drawn of

> The Sylvan Scenes of Herds and Flocks,
> And fruitful Plains and barren Rocks;
> Of shallow Brooks that flow'd so clear,
> The Bottom did the Top appear;
> Of deeper too and ampler Flouds,
> Which as in Mirrors, shew'd the Woods;
> Of lofty Trees with Sacred Shades,
> And Perspectives of pleasant Glades....

This pleasing little passage, in a manner which we do not usually associate with him, leads on to other topics, and finally to a description of the Day of Judgement, in which four lines about 'rattling bones' and 'skeletons' recall old tombstones and monuments. Had these lines been omitted, as they can be without harming the run of the sense, the picture of the Resurrection would escape our modern censures, though it would still remain dated. After the magnificent first stanza, the poem cannot escape the criticism, which has to be made on Pindaric odes in general, that the verse sometimes fails to show a clear reason for its changes. But the freedom in the structure of the stanzas allowed for varied effects, and Dryden sought for these.

This memorial ode was shortly followed by an ode, *On the Marriage of the Fair and Vertuous Lady, Mrs. Anastasia Stafford*, the daughter of a Roman Catholic family which is not otherwise known to have had any association with Dryden. It may have been his first poem after his conversion. Perhaps unfinished, it was first published in 1813 in the volume entitled *Tixall*

Poetry, and though it is not included in most editions of Dryden's works, the style shows it to be his. I mention it now only as further evidence of his occupation, during a brief period, with Pindaric verse.

The two odes for St Cecilia's day, which come after this brief period, are not to be called Pindaric odes because the verse varies from stanza to stanza. They were written to be sung, and their form had to be suited to the accompaniment of strings and wind instruments. The wonder is that they are so good. Their titles say 'Song', not 'Ode'.

A musical festival in honour of St Cecilia—the patron saint of music, whose day is 22 November—was held annually from 1683, when the music was composed by Purcell, and in 1687 Dryden was asked to supply the words. He took as his subject the power of music, and again he gives us a great opening:

> From Harmony, from heav'nly Harmony,
> This universal Frame began. . .*etc.*

He then suggests in stanzas of different quality, for he has the instrumentalists in view, the sound and scope of the trumpet with its loud clangour, the soft complaining flute, the warbling lute, the sharp violins, and lastly the greatest of instruments, of which St Cecilia was taken to be the inventress, the organ with its 'vocal breath'. Finally, the Grand Chorus returns to the theme of the opening. The variations in the metre are all designed. Each stanza had a clear purpose and fits into the scheme.

Yet we have to say that we cannot read it all without thinking, not of the instruments (we are asked to think of them) but of the instrumentalists in the act of performing, and that is one reason why, in Johnson's words, it is 'lost in the splendour of the second ode', which, again on invitation, Dryden wrote ten years later—*Alexander's Feast*. We can read *Alexander's Feast* without thinking that it was written to be performed; its word-music is sufficient for us. And there is another reason for its superiority. It has a human interest. The power of music is shown in its effects on one person, and this power is exerted by one musician. As Timotheus touches his lyre Alexander assumes the god, then relaxes in the joys of Bacchus, fights all his battles o'er again, muses on the various turns of chance and pities a fallen foe

> Fallen, fallen, fallen, fallen
> Fallen from his high estate,

passes from pity to love, and finally is roused from love to revenge. Timotheus

> Could swell the soul to rage, or kindle soft desire.

The theme of the poem is as happy as the execution is masterly. This great ode is completely devoid of the sentimental element—I use the word in no debased sense—which we find in the great odes of the nineteenth century. That may not be a deficiency, but it may help to explain why, as much as any of his works, *Alexander's Feast* has had a varied reputation. Not many nowadays assent to the praises which it won from Gray, and Johnson, and Scott. But in the eighteenth century Goldsmith had his doubts about it when he said 'this Ode has been more applauded, perhaps, than it has been felt', though he added that it 'gives its beauties rather at a third, or fourth, than at a first, perusal'.[1]

Alexander's Feast was written in 1697, the year in which Dryden completed his Virgil. He was then aged

[1] *The Beauties of English Poesy* (1767), vol. i, p. 119.

sixty-six. But he pressed on to new work, and three years later, in the last year of his life, gave us his *Fables*. In the Preface to that volume he said—

What Judgment I had, increases rather than diminishes; and Thoughts, such as they are, come crowding in so fast upon me, that my only Difficulty is to chuse or to reject; to run them into Verse, or to give them the other Harmony of Prose: I have so long studied and practis'd both, that they are grown into a Habit, and become familiar to me.

The *Fables* is a collection of his later verse. After he had finished his *Aeneid* he tried the first book of the *Iliad*, and thought that he would have been better advised to have translated Homer instead of Virgil. Homer led him to think of the Trojan War as described in the *Metamorphoses*. Ovid in turn brought Chaucer into his mind, and him, too, he translated 'into our language as it is now refined'. And from Chaucer he was led to think of Boccaccio, and of doing as Chaucer had done in making stories that he had read in Italian or French the basis of original tales. He based three tales on Boccaccio, and these may have suggested *Fables* as the title to the volume. But he also included other poems that he had recently written. And, following his long-established habit, he wrote a preface—a very important preface. Altogether it is a volume of great richness. Its arrangement deserves attention. The translations are not grouped together by their authors, but intermingled, nor are the original tales kept by themselves. Dryden expected the reader to pass easily from Chaucer to Ovid, to Homer, to an original tale, and back to Chaucer.[1]

[1] Unfortunately this arrangement was abandoned by Dryden's editors, but it was restored in the edition by G. R. Noyes, 1909.

In the year 1700, when Chaucer was read in bad texts, Dryden grants him equal treatment with classical authors. Because we may not like to see Chaucer modernized we must not be blind to the novelty of this equal treatment, and to its boldness.

To us who read Chaucer in good texts, these adaptations to the taste of another age cannot make a strong appeal. We must regret the loss of much of Chaucer's simplicity and directness. The humour becomes less gentle; the additions are in a different style. But the pleasure which Dryden found in rewriting Chaucer is unmistakable. *Palamon and Arcite* in particular has undeniable merits—almost, as Scott said, the merit of originality. Even Professor Skeat declared in print that the rendering of the non-Chaucerian *Flower and the Leaf* is 'finer than the original'.

We are too apt to forget that Dryden's contemporaries were not as familiar as we are with the originals, and that Dryden undertook these modernizations with the purpose of making Chaucer better known. It was an act of service, an act of piety to 'the father of English poetry'. 'I have translated some parts of his works', he says, 'only that I might perpetuate his memory, or at least refresh it amongst my countrymen.' And he undertook them in the face of opposition or indifference. 'I find', he says, 'some people are offended that I have turned these tales into modern English; because they think them unworthy of my pains and look on Chaucer as a dry old-fashioned wit, not worth reviving,... Mr. Cowley himself was of that opinion.' He is often condemned for not recognizing the perfection of Chaucer's verse; but in the text which he used—Speght's edition of 1687—we continually come on lines which are, as he said, 'lame for want of half a foot'. Dryden was not a textualist. He lived before textual criticism had spread to English poetry. He accepted the text that he was given, and he was right in saying, on the evidence of this text, that Chaucer's versification was very irregular. 'The verse of Chaucer, I confess, is not harmonious to us'; and we should say the same if we were placed as he was. But this impediment makes it the more remarkable that he should have gone so far as to match Chaucer with the great story-teller of classical literature and to show why, in days when Ovid's reputation stood higher than it appears to do now, the preference must be given to Chaucer. This he does in his preface, and we may be certain that to the readers of the year 1700 no section of the preface was more unexpected. The whole passage on Chaucer is one of the great pronouncements of English criticism. It recalls the 'model of encomiastick criticism' which he had written over thirty years earlier. They are at the beginning and the end of his long career as a critic, in which he always spoke his mind freely, except when a patron was in view, and without fear. But there is this difference. In his praise of Shakespeare he gave heightened expression to what others were thinking; in his praise of Chaucer he broke through received opinion, and about Chaucer's essential merits, as distinct from his versification, he said what we all say now.

Dryden's greatness as a critic is to be judged, first of all, by such a passage as this. But for a true estimate of his greatness we have to take into account, not only his originality and his insight in appreciation, but also the new ideas with which he enriched the functions of English criticism. We have seen the importance in this respect of the Essay *Of Dramatick Poesie*. That work had many

novelties which were to be made common by his successors. But we never know where he will not point the way
to what is coming. Even in his 'Life of Plutarch' he gives
us, I believe, the first deliberate examination in English
of an author's prose style. In the preface to the *Fables*
all is overshadowed by the praise of Chaucer, but he
foresaw an occupation which was to be indulged in, for
good or ill, by many critics of the eighteenth and nineteenth centuries, and with which we may sometimes
think that we have become too familiar:

Milton was the Poetical Son of *Spencer*, and Mr. *Waller* of
Fairfax; for we have our Lineal Descents and Clans, as well as
other Families.

Dryden says 'Clans' and 'Families'; but here we are at
the beginning of the division of our poets into 'Schools'.

In his original tales he again broke new ground. He
was always breaking new ground—to the very end of his
life that was his way. He was too vigorous and restless
by nature to be content with continuing to do what he
had already done well. With the example of Chaucer
before him, he turns to telling a story in verse. 'I found',
he says, 'that I had a soul congenial to his'. The fable of
the swallows in *The Hind and the Panther* may be regarded as a preliminary exercise, but it was written
before he studied Chaucer and while he still looked to
Ovid, and it is incidental in an argumentative poem. His
three tales are all very well told. When they are read to
us, we have no difficulty in following them. The points
are taken at once, and the attention is held. And when
we read them to ourselves, we continually come upon
passages which we read again to renew our pleasure in
them—passages which call up a picture of the country

(he has more description showing first-hand knowledge than is often supposed) or of a social scene or of a storm on land or at sea, or passages containing observations on human nature and ordinary experiences. The matter is varied, but the main lines of the story are clear. I know that if anyone were to read to you the story of Cymon, the handsome dolt who could not be taught, and who, though an eldest son, was sent by his father to drudge on a farm, where

> He trudg'd along unknowing what he sought,
> And whistled as he went, for want of Thought,

who falls in love, and has his mind awakened by love, and then determines that he must be educated, and so

> sought a Tutor of his own accord,
> And study'd Lessons he before abhorr'd,

and thereafter was

> More fam'd for Sense, for courtly Carriage more,
> Than for his brutal Folly known before—

—I know that if anyone read this to you, you would wish to hear more. And if you did hear more you would get a very good shipwreck and a parade of the 'rude militia', the very primitive equivalent of our excellent Home Guard:

> The Country rings around with loud Alarms,
> And raw in Fields the rude Militia swarms;
> Mouths without Hands; maintain'd at vast Expence,
> In Peace a Charge, in War a weak Defence:
> Stout once a Month they march, a blust'ring Band,
> And ever, but in times of Need, at hand:

> This was the Morn when issuing on the Guard,
> Drawn up in Rank and File they stood prepar'd
> Of seeming Arms to make a short essay,
> Then hasten to be Drunk, the Business of the Day.

Varied matter, and so arranged as to keep our attention
alert; but the theme of the story is this—

> Love never fails to master what he finds,
> But works a diff'rent way in diff'rent Minds,
> The Fool enlightens, and the Wise he blinds.

All three tales are of love. Wordsworth seems to have
preferred *Sigismonda and Guiscardo*, of which he said in
a letter to Scott that with all its defects 'it is a noble
poem'. Scott was attracted by the apparition and the
'beauties of the terrific order' in *Theodore and Honoria*,
and so was Byron; Gray placed it with *Absalom and
Achitophel* in the first rank of Dryden's poems. These
tales were written as Dryden was approaching the age
of seventy, when, as he said, in *Cymon and Iphigenia*, 'The
power of beauty still inspires my wit'. They seemed to
Wordsworth to be 'the most poetical' of Dryden's
poems. Hazlitt thought them 'upon the whole the most
popular of his works'. Keats showed the effects of his
reading of them in his *Lamia*. Wordsworth, Scott, Byron,
Hazlitt, Keats—and how many of us are familiar with the
Fables now? For the last hundred years what has been
thought of first at the mention of his name is satire. That
is because of his pre-eminence in satire. But let me
again remind you that his satires belong to a short period
of his long career; and let me add that we should not
allow their brilliance to distract our attention from other
poems in which like pre-eminence cannot be claimed for
him. No one would claim it for him in the tale. There
is Chaucer who after five hundred years still remains

the unchallenged master. But whom would we place second? That is a difficult question, to which we can predict several answers. But the claims of Dryden would have to be considered.

I know that I should speak of his epistle 'To my Honour'd Kinsman John Driden of Chesterton' which is included in this volume of *Fables*, and with it I should group the epistles to Congreve and Sir Godfrey Kneller. The epistle allows the poet to pass from topic to topic — its nature, like that of the preface, is rambling—and Dryden was completely at his ease in it. Flicks of mordant satire are followed by passages of tenderness and affection, as in the epistle to Congreve where he says

> Oh that your Brows my Lawrel had sustain'd,
> Well had I been depos'd, if You had reign'd,

and calls upon him to

> Be kind to my Remains; and oh defend,
> Against your Judgment, your departed Friend.

They are more colloquial than Pope's, and more intimate, and they do not suffer by being less finished. It is a form of writing which has long been out of fashion, but it offers great opportunities, and I could wish that a modern poet would attempt to revive it.

But I pass on to speak, more briefly than I should have liked, about his prose. No one has written about it better than Johnson; I would even go further and say that no critic has yet written better about Dryden whether as prose-writer or poet than Johnson did in his *Life*.

The clauses [he says] are never balanced, nor the periods modelled; every word seems to drop by chance, though it falls into its proper place. Nothing is cold or languid; the whole is airy, animated, and vigorous.... Everything is excused by the play of images and the spriteliness of expression. Though all is easy, nothing is feeble; though all seem careless, there is nothing harsh; and though since his earlier works more than a century has passed, they have nothing yet uncouth or obsolete.

He who writes much will not easily escape a manner, such a recurrence of particular modes as may be easily noted. Dryden is always *another and the same*.

After this we may wonder why Johnson said that the young writer should give his days and nights to the study of Addison, not of Dryden. He thought that the ease and the seeming absence of care might mislead.

Congreve, who remembered Dryden's appeal to 'Be kind to my remains', brought out an edition of Dryden's *Dramatick Works* in 1717, and in the Dedication he wrote this sentence which has given some trouble—

I have heard him frequently own with Pleasure, that if he had any Talent for *English* Prose, it was owing to his having often read the Writings of the great Archbishop *Tillotson*.

On the face of it this is a manifest exaggeration, at the least, though we need not say that Dryden is incorrectly reported. He was writing good prose from a very early date. We need think only of the Essay *Of Dramatick Poesie*. But we cannot ignore the remark, especially as it was made 'frequently'.

In the preface to *Religio Laici* Dryden says:

I have us'd the necessary Precaution, of showing this Paper [i.e. the poem] before it was Publish'd to a judicious and learned Friend, a Man indefatigably zealous in the service of the Church and State: and whose Writings have highly deserv'd of both.

This man was Tillotson, preacher at Lincoln's Inn and Canon of St Paul's before he was appointed Dean in 1680.

Dryden must have been familiar with his *Rule of Faith* (1666) and his early Sermons, where the same ground is traversed as in *Religio Laici*. We know too little about their personal relations, but they must have been on close terms of friendship when Dryden submitted to him the manuscript of his poem. It may well be that his writings, and perhaps his preaching, had drawn Dryden's attention to little niceties of style.

Dryden's first reference to a nicety which he had neglected is found in 1672 in his ' Defence of the Epilogue' to *The Conquest of Granada* where after pointing out that 'the preposition in the end of the sentence' is a common fault with Ben Jonson, he adds—'and which I have but lately observed in my own writings'. He might have begun his reading of Tillotson by then, for, as we saw, he had his religious difficulties while he was writing his heroic plays. But the best evidence of his care for his style is provided by the revised edition of the Essay *Of Dramatick Poesie*, which for some unknown reason he brought out in 1684. This edition contains over a hundred alterations which are merely verbal. In general they aim at improving the rhythm by giving a firmer ending to a sentence or a clause. The alteration which is made most frequently affects the place of the preposition. For instance 'people you speak of' is altered to 'people of whom you speak'; or the preposition may be omitted, as when a paragraph which had ended with 'can arrive at' is made to end with 'can reasonably hope to reach'. Somehow Dryden had realized that a sentence had better not end with an unaccented monosyllable. Now I suggest that these alterations contain the clue to his professed debt to Tillotson. The style of Tillotson is clear and easy, but is free from the colloquial placing of the preposition, and I am ready to believe that it drew his attention to this and other little points affecting the turn of a phrase. But that his debt to Tillotson was greater than that—No! Dryden's prose is much more muscular than Tillotson's and rivets our attention much more strongly. It would have been wholly in keeping with the generosity of his nature—for he was as generous in his acknowledgements to a friend as he could be bitter in his treatment of an enemy—to have made the most of a very little. He must have known as well as we do that the 'harmony' of his prose, and its clarity, and its vivacity, were not derived from the mere workmanlike efficiency of Tillotson's.

These talks on Dryden have now to end. For over thirty years he was the acknowledged leader in poetry and criticism, and had he lived into the New Age which he hailed but did not see, his writings must still have been charged with his ardent and untiring spirit. The New Age paid him the honour which he would have liked best as the reward for his long and agitated career of continuous activity. He became the teacher of the young poets; Pope admitted that he had 'learned versification wholly from Dryden's works'. But great as was their debt to him in the formal aspects of verse, and in the choice of language, they owed him another and a greater debt. He had provided the stimulus which comes with the admiration of force, and ease, and inexhaustible vigour. It is a stimulus which he still exerts on us.

INDEX

Absalom and Achitophel, 46, 49–55, 66, 86; Part II, 59
Addison, Joseph, 48, 88
Aesop, 64
Alexander's Feast, 80
All for Love, 40–3, 44
Annus Mirabilis, 8–11, 12
Aristotle, *Poetics*, 18, 44
Arthurian romance, 45
Astræa Redux, 6–8
Aubrey, John, 36, 37
Aureng-zebe, 24, 32–4, 44

Bede, 45
Bentley, Richard, 71
Bethel, Sir Slingsby, 54
Black Prince, proposed epic, 45
Blackmore, Sir Richard, 45
Blank verse, 10, 15, 42–3
Boccaccio, 81
Boileau-Despréaux, Nicolas, 50
Bridges, Robert, 4, 17
Browne, Sir Thomas, 62
Buckingham, Duke of, 51
Butler, Samuel, 55
Byron, Lord, 86

Chapman's *Homer*, 72
Charles II, 6, 53, 56, 57, 62, 76
Chaucer, 81–4, 86
Christie, William Dougal, 2
Coleridge, Samuel Taylor, 21
Collier, Jeremy, 78
Comedy of Manners, 26
Congreve, William, 26, 68, 74; epistle to, 87; edition of Dryden's dramas, 88
Conquest of Granada, The, 27–33, 34, 89
Corneille, Pierre, 17–19, 24, 40; *Discours Dramatiques*, 18

Cowley, Abraham, *Pindaric Odes*, 73–4; on Chaucer, 82
Creech, Thomas, 68
Cromwell, Heroic Stanzas to the memory of, 5, 6, 9
Cymon and Iphigenia, 85–6

Daniel, Samuel, 40
D'Aubignac, François Hédelin, Abbé, 18
Davenant, Sir William, 10, 11
Davies, Sir John, 10
Denham, Sir John, 71, 73
Donne, John, 21
Dorset, Earl of, 67
Douglas, Gavin, 71
Dramatick Poesie, Essay Of, 12–22, 23, 40, 60, 61, 66, 67, 83, 88, 89
Driden, John, To my Honour'd Kinsman, 87
Drummond, William, of Hawthornden, 45
DRYDEN
    Debt to Trinity College, 1, 2; poet laureate, 11; attitude to political parties, 6, 58–9; shareholder in Theatre Royal, 24; Comedies, 24–6; Heroic Plays, 27–35; personal relations with Milton, 36–8; 'imitates' Shakespeare, 40–3; tires of drama, 24, 44; thinks of an epic, 44–6; turns to satire, 46–9; political satires, 49–60; religious poems, 60–6; becomes a Roman Catholic, 62, 67; loses the laureateship, 67; his old age, 67; translations, 67–73; odes, 73–80; tales,

91

DRYDEN (cont.)
81–6; epistles, 87; always breaking new ground, 84; 'judgment increases', 81; descriptions of country scenes, 65, 78, 84–5; a master of the opening, 66, 69, 77, 79

VERSE: his quatrains not elegiac, 10–11; stress varied in couplets, 33, 65; his blank verse, 42–3; his excellent ear, 39; practice required, 7

PROSE: 'the other harmony', 81; debt to Tillotson, 88; corrections, 89; Johnson on its merits, 87

CRITICISM: mostly Prefaces, 12; like studio talk, 25; of Shakespeare, 19–20, 83; of Spenser, 45, 71; of Donne, 21; of Milton, 38–40; of contemporary poetry, 21; its new ideas, 83–4

Elizabethan drama, 14, 16
Epic, project of, 44–6; essay on (dedication of *Virgil*), 44, 70–1
Etherege, Sir George, 26

Fables, 65, 86
Fitzgerald, Edward, 72
Flecknoe, Richard, 48–9; *Short Discourse of the English Stage*, 17. And see *MacFlecknoe*
Flower and the Leaf, The, 82

Gascoigne, George, *Steele Glas*, 10
Goldsmith, Oliver, 80
Gray, Thomas, 10, 74, 80, 86

Halifax, Marquess of, 54
Hazlitt, William, 86
Heinsius, Daniel, 18
Hero and Leander, 34
Heroic play, 27–32

Hind and the Panther, The, 63–6, 67, 84
Homer, 70, 71, 81
Horace, 50, 73–6
Hudibras, 55

Indian Emperor, The, 14, 15

James II, 62, 63, 67
Johnson, Samuel, 4, 11, 20, 39; *The Vanity of Human Wishes*, 69; Preface to Shakespeare, 20; *Life of Dryden*, 87; on Dryden's poems, 69, 79, 80; on Dryden's prose, 87–8
Jonson, Ben, 18, 19, 45, 72, 74, 89; *The Silent Woman*, 19–20
'Jotham', 54
Juvenal, 50, 68–9, 73

Keats, John, 33, 75, 78, 86
Killigrew, Mrs. Anne, To the memory of, 77
King Arthur (opera), 45
Kneller, Sir Godfrey, epistle to, 87

La Mesnardière, Jules de, 18
Laureateship, 11, 57, 67
Le Bossu, René, 44

MacFlecknoe, 17, 47–9, 56, 66
Mackenzie, Sir George, 62
Malone, Edmond, 2
Marlowe, Christopher, 34
Marriage A-la-Mode, 26
Marvell, Andrew, 35, 55
May, Thomas, 40
Medal, The, 57–8, 60
Medal of John Bayes, The, 59
Milton, 15, 45, 84; *Paradise Lost*, 9, 10, 35, 36, 63; relations with Dryden, 36–8; 'rhyme was not his talent', 38–40
Miscellany Poems (1684), 47
Monitor, The, 37
Monmouth, Duke of, 49, 53

INDEX

Oates, Titus, 54
Oldham, John, 7, 47, 55; *To the Memory of*, 7, 56
Ovid, 68, 72, 81, 84
Oxford, 1

Palamon and Arcite, 81, 82
Pepys, Samuel, 14
Persius, 50
Phillips, Edward, 23, 24
Pitt, Christopher, 71
Plutarch, Life of, 2, 84
Pope, Alexander, 8, 48, 49, 71, 87, 90
Prologues and Epilogues, 1, 27, 32, 47
Purcell, Henry, 45, 79

Racine, Jean, 24; *Phèdre*, 40
Rehearsal, The, 29, 30, 46, 50
Religio Laici, 31, 60–2, 63, 66, 88, 89
Religio Medici, 62
Religio Stoici, 62
Roscommon, Earl of, 72
Royal Society, 13
Rymer, Thomas, 40

St Cecilia's Day, Song for, 79
Saintsbury, George, 4
Sandys's *Ovid*, 79
Satire, Dryden's innovations in, 49–57: 'fine raillery', 50; *Discovery concerning Satire*, 39, 50, 73
Satyrs upon the Jesuits, 55
Scaliger, J. C., *Poetics*, 18
Scott, Sir Walter, *Life of Dryden*, 2; *Marmion*, 4; *The Pirate*, 4; on Dryden's proposed epic, 46, 63, 80, 82, 86
Sedley, Sir Charles, 40
Settle, Elkanah, 46, 59

Shadwell, Thomas, 46–9, 59–60
Shaftesbury, Earl of, 49, 52, 58
Shakespeare, William, 14, 15, 19, 20, 23; *Antony and Cleopatra*, 40–2
Sigismonda and Guiscardo, 86
Skeat, Walter W., 82
Speght's *Chaucer*, 82
Spenser, 38, 84; *The Faerie Queene*, 44–5; *Mother Hubberd's Tale*, 64; Dryden's debt to, 71
Stafford, Mrs. Anastasia, On the marriage of, 78
State of Innocence, The, 35, 36

Tamburlaine, 35
Tennyson, Lord, 11
Thrale, Mrs Hester Lynch, 32
Threnodia Augustalis, 76–7
Tillotson, John, archbishop, 88–90
Tixall Poetry, 78
Tonson, Jacob, 68
Translation, problems of, 71–3
Trinity College, Cambridge, 1, 2
True Widow, A, Dryden's prologue, 47
Tyrannick Love, 27, 29, 31

Unity of Time, 10 2

Verrall, Arthur Woolgar, 2, 3, 36
Vindication of the Duke of Guise, 59
Virgil, 67, 70–3, 80, 81
Virtuoso, The, Shadwell's epilogue, 46–7

Waller, Edmund, 6, 37, 71, 84
William III, 68
Wordsworth, William, 74, 86
Wycherley, William, 26

'Zimri', 50, 51, 53